The Athlete and Their Mechanisms of Defense

This important book explores the way athletes use defense mechanisms and coping skills to manage both the internal and external stress faced in competitive sport. Covering a range of case studies across various sports, the text showcases a taxonomy of immature, neurotic and mature defenses available to the athlete and describes the benefits and drawbacks of each.

A clear introductory section defines what defense mechanisms are and how they impact performance such as shame, anxiety, despair, memories of previous losses or fantasies about winning. Applying a psychoanalytic approach in line with the ideas of Sigmund Freud, Anna Freud, Fenichel, Leo Rangel, George Valliant and many others, the author uses each case study to connect the defense mechanism under investigation with the world of the athlete. Focused on delivering research-based evidence, the book helps readers deepen their understanding of the different types of defense mechanisms used by athletes across the globe, as the author explains what causes them and recommends techniques for developing effective coping skills. Each chapter of the book also includes a reflective section that challenges the reader to think about how they can help athletes to grow and develop healthy defense mechanisms in any stage of their career.

This invaluable text is geared toward the practitioners, researchers, psychoanalysts and students in sport psychology who wish to look more deeply into why athletes struggle. It is also an ideal resource for athletes interested in understanding ways to cope with the unrelenting, exciting and at times overwhelming pressure of competitive sports.

Dr. Tom Ferraro is a psychoanalyst in private practice who works with both amateur and professional athletes and teams. Working in the New York metropolitan area, he is also an author, award-winning syndicated columnist and has been featured in the *New York Times*, *The Wall Street Journal* and the *London Times*.

The Athlete and Their Mechanisms of Defense
A Psychoanalytic Approach to Sport Psychology

Tom Ferraro

Cover image: CasarsaGuru via Getty Images

First published 2025
by Routledge
605 Third Avenue, New York, NY 10158

and by Routledge
4 Park Square, Milton Park, Abingdon, Oxon, OX14 4RN

Routledge is an imprint of the Taylor & Francis Group, an informa business

© 2025 Tom Ferraro

The right of Tom Ferraro to be identified as author of this work has been asserted in accordance with sections 77 and 78 of the Copyright, Designs and Patents Act 1988.

All rights reserved. No part of this book may be reprinted or reproduced or utilised in any form or by any electronic, mechanical, or other means, now known or hereafter invented, including photocopying and recording, or in any information storage or retrieval system, without permission in writing from the publishers.

Trademark notice: Product or corporate names may be trademarks or registered trademarks, and are used only for identification and explanation without intent to infringe.

ISBN: 978-1-032-56596-5 (hbk)
ISBN: 978-1-032-56595-8 (pbk)
ISBN: 978-1-003-43627-0 (ebk)

DOI: 10.4324/9781003436270

Typeset in Sabon
by codeMantra

Contents

Preface	*viii*
Introduction	1
1 Defense Mechanisms Used by Athletes	6
2 Why Defense Mechanisms Must Be Addressed Prior to Teaching Coping Skills?	12
3 Emotional Breakdowns in Athletes: Why They Happen and What to Do About Them	17

PART 1
Immature Defenses — 23

4 Denial Mechanisms in an Aging Athlete	24
5 Acting Out, Impulsivity and Drug Use in Athletes	29
6 Grandiosity, Self-idealization and Narcissism in the Athlete	34
7 Depersonalization in a Golfer	38
8 Autistic Fantasies in a Long-Distance Swimmer	42
9 Perfectionism or the Splitting Defense in Athletes	46
10 Superstitious Behavior Used by the Regressed Athlete	51
11 Regression in a Professional Soccer Team	55
12 Somatization in Athletes	60

| 13 | Scapegoating and Splitting in Professional Teams | 67 |
| 14 | Identification with the Aggressor as a Tool to Suppress Anxiety | 73 |

PART 2
The Neurotic Defenses   77

15	Displacement of Anger into a Spouse	78
16	Repression and Reaction Formation in Asian Athletes	81
17	Overcompensation: Turning Inferiority into Superiority in a LPGA Golfer	86
18	Doubting in Athletes and the Intellectualization Defense	90
19	The Undoing Defense: Why Athletes Choke	94
20	Isolation of Affect Defense in Athletes	99
21	Dissociation in Sports	103
22	Reaction Formation: The Problem of Being Mr. Nice Guy	107
23	The Yips in Golf as an Example of Repression	112

PART 3
The Mature Defenses   117

24	Counterphobia or Why Athletes Compete	118
25	The Value of Self-Observation for Athletes	122
26	Altruistic Surrender in Sports or Why Athletes Give Away Leads	125
27	The Anticipation Defense as the Definitive Pre-Game Routine	129
28	Asceticism and the Renunciation of Pleasure in a Long-Distance Cyclist	133
29	How Athletes Use Humor to Cope with Stress	138
30	Suppression Used to Manage Competitive Anxiety	141

31 Sublimation, Aggression and Winning	144
32 Sublimation of the Sexual Impulse in Sports	148

PART 4
Odds and Ends 153

33 The Weakening of Defense Mechanisms with Age	154
34 Meditation and Prayer as a Way to Find the Zone	157
35 Using a "Higher Power" as a Coping Mechanism in Sports	162
36 Mental Health versus Mental Illness in Athletes	166
37 The Problem of Prescription Drug Use in Athletes	172
38 Depression Used as a Defense by Athletes Who Fear Failure	176
39 Cultural Differences in the Use of Defenses	180
40 Concluding Remarks on Ways to Identify Defenses in Athletes	188
Index	*195*

Preface

When I was asked to write a book about how athletes use their defenses to cope with stress, I accepted the challenge gladly. This was an opportunity to explore an uncharted area of sport psychology, how athletes naturally cope with their performance anxiety. Much has been written about the many coping skills that athletes need to be taught but virtually nothing about how they naturally dealt with competitive stress. This book is not intended to be a complete review of depth sport psychology. My last book "Unpacking Depth Sport Psychology: Case Studies in the Unconscious" provided an overall view of how to work with the athlete using a psychodynamic approach. This book focuses exclusively on the athletes' defense mechanisms.

The fact that you're reading this suggests that you are interested in the mind of the athlete. The athlete's mind works on two levels, a conscious and an unconscious one. The unconscious has power that affects every athlete's performance. The unique feature of depth sport psychology is that it addresses the athlete's unconscious. Its methodology includes but is not limited to the coping methods taught in cognitive behavior therapy. This book offers a taxonomic view of the defense mechanisms used by athletes and is offered as a guide to those who want to help the athlete improve. The broader psychoanalytic concepts and techniques used to treat athletes such as super ego function, free association, dream analysis, transference, countertransference and resistance were addressed in my first book.

Every sport psychologist knows how difficult it is to change an attitude, perception, mood or mindset. Many a sport psychology book promises a cure for performance issues through the application of goal setting, deep breathing, autogenics, thinking positively, cognitive behavior therapy or visualization. and visualizing targets. Most of the elite athlete I know have been taught these techniques before they left high school, yet they continue to struggle emotionally. The hope is that the athlete's performance woes can be fixed with relative ease and within a short period of time. This is a myth. The reality is it's exceedingly tough to make changes in an athlete's mindset because their underlying conflicts are out of awareness and dictated by irrational and childlike perceptions. The 'behavior modifiers' seek to circumvent these unconscious defense mechanisms without an understanding of what the defenses do and without regard for their value. I believe the field has reached a fork in the road. It is now time to take the next step and explore the athlete's unconscious.

As a psychoanalyst, I work with professional and amateur athletes on ways to help them feel less stress and regain joy and pride in themselves. I've undertaken to write this book because the field needs a paradigm shift if it expects to remain relevant. The athlete's defenses function like a skin or a suit of armor which enables them to remain calm and poised while under stress. To my knowledge, there has not been a single book written on this subject. In fact, I couldn't find a single reference to the term defense mechanism in any of the standard sport psychology textbooks now being used in undergraduate or graduate courses.

Nearly every professional athlete I've worked with have physical gifts, natural talent and a highly developed work ethic but that is not enough. To win, one must be able to screen out distractions, cope with stress, remain confident, tap into aggression and manage anxiety. When athletes lose power, chokes, is prone to self-defeat, it is due to a failure in their defense mechanisms.

This book explores the most common defenses athletes use to cope with competitive stress and threats to self-esteem. I will explore which defenses are most effective, which are not effective and I will present case studies demonstrating how their defenses work, why they sometimes shatter and what to do about it. My thinking has been influenced by psychoanalytic pioneers such as Sigmund Freud, Anna Freud and George Vaillant as well as contemporaries like Phebe Cramer (2006) Farhad Dalal (2018), Christopher Bollas, Dan Dervin, Mark Nesti and David Burston. I think all of these luminaries would agree that it's time for a change in sport psychology. My guess is that the change must be by helping the athlete look deeply within.

Tom Ferraro, Ph.D. December 9, 2023
Long Island, New York

References

Cramer, P. (2006) *Protecting the Self, Defense Mechanisms in Action*. The Guilford Press.
Dilal, F. (2018) *CBT: The Cognitive Behavioural Tsunami*. Routledge.
Gardner, F. & Moore, Z. (2006) *Clinical Sport Psychology*. Human Kinetics.
Kuhn, T. (1962) *The Structure of Scientific Revolutions*. The Guilford Press.
Lawrence, D.H. (1923) *Studies in Classic American Literature*. Penguin Books.
O'Donohue, W. & Krasner, K. (1995) Theories in Behavior Therapy: Philosophical and Historical Contexts. In *Theories of Behavior Therapy: Exploring Behavior Change* (Eds. W. O'Donohue & K. Krasner). American Psychological Association, 1–22.

Introduction

"Temet Nosce" (Know Thyself)
                Inscribed on the Temple of Apollo 500 B.C.

The failure to address the athlete's unconscious has produced a weakness in the way sport psychology is currently conducted. For the last 70 years, the field of sport psychology has embraced the cognitive-behavioral approach to treating the athlete's performance woes. The results have been less than impressive (Gardner & Moore, 2006). I have worked as a sport psychologist for the last 25 years, and at the beginning of my career, I assiduously applied state-of-the-art behavioral techniques to help athletes cope with their anxiety, yips, anger, lack of focus, slumps, self-doubt and despair. Overtime, I came to realize that cognitive-behavioral techniques were quite weak in their ability to deal with the stress the competitive athlete must face. It also became very apparent that the repetitive application of self-talk mantras or deep breathing tips becomes boring, inane and essentially meaningless within short order. I once asked Albert Ellis, the founder of rational emotive therapy, how he was able to cope with repetitive nature of his techniques and he laughed at me and said "don't bother me with such questions." For sport psychology to be used by athletes, it must be engaging and interesting to them and not mechanical, superficial or meaningless to them personally. Sport psychology sessions had better be interesting for both the athlete and the therapist or it's quickly abandoned.

It is time for a paradigm shift in sport psychology and Thomas Kuhn remarked, paradigm shifts are necessary for the field to grow but they are always resisted (Kuhn, 1962). This book contains an introduction to the psychoanalytic approach to performance problems, an approach that enables the athlete to become freer, more spontaneous and happier both on and off the playing field. I will demonstrate how the athlete's underlying conflicts impact their performance through case studies from my practice. It is by not easy to gain access to our unconscious, and the therapist needs special training. In addition, the athlete must not be too disturbed, must not be sociopathic, must have good intelligence, must have some level of trust and be somewhat introspective or curious about his inner workings.

Depth sport psychology seeks to improve the athlete's understanding of him or herself and seeks out the meaning behind symptoms and performance problems. This is in stark contrast to the cognitive-behavioral approach taken by most sport psychologists. The basic attitude of behavior modifiers is seen in the following anecdote. I received my Ph.D. for SUNY Stony Brook whose faculty included some of the founders of behavior therapy. I was taught by Leonard Krasner, Herbert Kaye, Marv Goldfried and Dan O'Leary. One of my first-year classes was on Theories of Language Acquisition taught by Dr. Russ Whitehurst. The course relied on reinforcement theory to explain language acquisition in children, and when I asked about the function of meaning or semantics in language acquisition, Dr. Whitehurst said "Meaning of the words had no relevance in language acquisition." Behavior modifiers like observables whereas psychoanalysts like the unobservables, those things which lie beneath.

The way that athletes avoid being aware of what lies beneath is by developing and using their defense mechanisms. Most people are familiar with defense mechanisms like denial, regression, dissociation, somatization, repression, suppression, rationalization, humor, sublimation and altruism. This book will outline the way defense mechanisms are used by athletes as their primary way to cope with competitive stress. All of this is done unconsciously, and anxiety is only ever felt when defenses begin to break down The athlete's defense mechanisms protect them from a breakthrough of uncomfortable emotions coming from within or from without. Up until the present, sport psychology has been based upon cognitive/behavioral theory, a theory which states that reinforcement of different behaviors, the use of self-talk and the teaching of coping skills can alter the athlete's performance woes without reference to unconscious matters. One of behaviorisms founding fathers was B.F. Skinner who suggested that the unconscious mind ought not be considered when working with patients (Skinner, 1938).

In this book, we will be investigating the defense mechanisms used by my patients who are highly skilled professional and Olympic level athletes struggling with performance or emotional problems. Much has been written about how to teach coping skills to the athlete but very little has been written about the way athletes use their own naturally developed defense mechanisms to cope with stress.

Sigmund Freud (Freud, 1961) along with his daughter Anna Freud (Freud, 1966) established the theory of defense mechanisms to help explain how we manage our drives of aggression and sexuality. Since the world of sports requires the channeling of aggression, there is evident advantage to studying the athlete's defense mechanisms to observe how the athlete either represses or releases aggression.

The coping skills currently taught provide a potpourri of tips all of which are based upon different theories (classical conditioning, operant conditioning, cognitive theory, acceptance theory). This has resulted in a hodgepodge of interventions that often do not hold together theoretically. There are more than 400 schools of psychotherapy (O'Donohue & Krasner, 1995) and the almost random use of these techniques leads to confusion and chaos in the field. In contrast to this, depth sport psychology is based on a single theory called psychoanalysis with a unified and relatively simple theory (see text box below).

> ***FREUD ON THE UNCONSIOUS: Freud's most significant discovery was that the unconscious exists and that it takes energy to repress and defend against the wishes, impulses and memories contained within the unconscious. As one resolves their unconscious problems, there will be less self-defeat, more access to energy and greater spontaneity and problem-solving ability. As unconscious problems are resolved, the energy expended in repressing or defending against them is released and the athlete regains this energy, called libido, which results in more energy to perform. However, as Freud pointed out, society on the whole has a great fear and dislike of the psychoanalyst (Civilization and its Discontents). The popularity of the Oscar winning film "The Silence of the Lambs" and the psychiatrist Hannibal Lector played by Anthony Hopkins attests to both the public's fear as well as its fascination with the analytic couch. Hannibal Lector was a charming, fascinating psychiatrist but watch out because he may bite your face off. Unfortunately, the bias against psychoanalysis is alive and well in the field of sports, and we will explore how this resistance is shown.

Athletes must continuously deal with pressure, large crowds, the media and expectations put upon them by fans and coaches. When their defenses fail them, they will feel anxiety which can disrupt performance. The cognitive-behavioral approach suggests that if one teaches mental coping skills, the athlete will rationally employ these tools to cope with their anxiety, pain, anger or disappointment. However, the assumption that athletes are rational beings in control of their thoughts and feelings is an unwarranted assumption. As one athlete told me today, "my coach keeps telling me to relax, not worry so much and chill out. Is he kidding me or what? He actually thinks I can control these things." If the athlete could employ logic and rational thinking, they would have done so long ago. There are deeply entrenched unconscious reasons for anxiety and self-defeat which are hidden behind defenses and housed within the unconscious. These reasons include guilt, exaggerated fears of losing, extreme neediness regarding winning, feelings of undeservingness, a weak self-image or fears that victory may lead to loneliness or separation. These reasons for self-defeat will remain a mystery to the athlete until they discover what they are. Performance enhancement will not be achieved through consciously based, easy to teach, mental skills training that are applied over 6–20 sessions (Dalal, 2018). Real progress can only be achieved by working ones way through their defense mechanisms.

The book will be divided into sections: athlete's immature defenses, the neurotic defenses and the mature defenses. The immature defenses include denial, drug use, self-idealization, depersonalization, autistic fantasy, superstitions, regression, somatization and identification with the aggressor. The neurotic defenses include repression, undoing, overcompensation, intellectualization, isolation, dissociation and reaction formation. The mature defenses include counterphobias, self-observation, altruistic surrender, anticipation, asceticism, humor, suppression and sublimation. A special ODDS & ENDS section will include the impact of aging on defense, meditation and a belief in a higher power as defense, mental health in the athlete, prescription drug use, depression as defense and cultural differences in the way defenses are used. Chapters will highlight different theorists or discuss how athletes from different countries employ their own cultures defense mechanisms, a heretofore unexplored but crucial topic.

Surprisingly, some of the more primitive defenses such as denial and identification with the aggressor can be extremely effective for the athlete whereas some of the more mature defenses like altruism, intellectualization and reaction formation are largely ineffective on the playing field. Each chapter will also include summary points, tips for best performance and recommended readings.

The outcomes observed in this book were not quick, easy or elegant. One of the dangers of reading case studies is that the work seems straightforward and prescriptive in nature. Depth sport psychology is not a cookie cutter approach where an athlete enters the therapy with a symptom that calls forth an intervention that is directly applied. The athlete's symptoms will include anxiety, despair, poor focus, exhaustion, psychosomatics, accident proneness, acting out, drug use, rage or some other form of neurotic self-defeat. What frequently occurs is that after a few sessions, the athlete will invariably feel a bit better and have some symptom relief. This is when most premature terminations occur. This is called the transference cure and is derived simply from the opportunity to ventilate feelings. But no real change has occurred and the symptoms will return within days of the premature termination. The job is to establish a working alliance which encourages trust and the overall creation of ego strength. No matter what intervention you might apply, resistance will always be felt, resistance to the work, resistance to giving up the symptoms and resistance to trust. There is a vast psychoanalytic literature on the concept of resistance, and there is no reason to assume that athletes are less resistant than normal patients (Milman & Goldman, 1987). The skilled and seasoned sport psychologist is aware of this and does their best to help the athlete work through their resistance so that the real cure can unfold over time.

In every case study, identities will be protected by changing elements like the sport being played, the sex or the age of the athlete, the nation of the athlete and many other elements making it impossible to identify the athlete.

References

Dalal, F. (2018) *CBT: The Cognitive Behavioural Tsunami*. Routledge.
Freud, S. (1961) *Civilization and Its Discontents Newly* (trans. J. Strachey). W. W. Norton and Company.
Freud, A. (1966) *The Ego and the Mechanisms of Defense* (trans. C. Baines). International University Press.
Gardener, F. & Moore, Z. (2006) *Clinical Sport Psychology*. Human Kinetics.
Kuhn, T. (1962) *The Structure of Scientific Revolutions*. University of Chicago Press.
Milman, D. & Goldman, G. (1987) *Techniques of Working with Resistance*. Jason Aronson.
O'Donohue, W. & Krasner, L. (1995) Theories in Behavior Therapy: Philosophical and Historical Contexts. In *Theories of Behavior Therapy: Exploring Behavior Change* (Eds. W. O'Donohue & L. Krasner) 1–22.
Skinner, B.F. (1938) *The Behavior of Organism: An Experimental Analysis*. Appleton Century.

1 Defense Mechanisms Used by Athletes

This chapter provides a brief overview of the most common defenses used by the athletes and will be categorized as primitive, neurotic or mature. Although the more primitive defenses are often described in a negative fashion, we will see that some primitive defenses are actually helpful during competitive play. However, the categorization of immature versus neurotic versus mature defense is useful. The immature defenses such as denial or autistic fantasy require much energy, distort reality too much and in the end lead to exhaustion and self-defeat. The more mature defenses like humor, sublimation or suppression require less expenditure of energy, produce less distortion and usually will lead to success or at least less self-defeat (Vaillant, 1992).

The primitive defenses are as follows:

a Denial: Denial is a primitive defense implying that the person is not recognizing reality. This defense is used as protection against overwhelming anxiety or despair. It is seen in situations that are beyond the athlete's control such as when an athlete ages but refuses to step away from a sport or when the athlete is told they have a serious injury but refuses to believe it. This defense is often dangerous and produces further injury (Chapter 5)
b Acting out: Acting out is common in athletes and is defined as the tendency to give in to an impulse to avoid tension. As an example, impulsive acting out in tennis produces many unforced errors due to the inability to wait patiently for an opening. The use of alcohol is an acting out in order to avoid the discomfort and tension felt by remaining sober (Chapter 6).
c Idealization of the self: The use of idealization of the self leads to perfectionism which is invariably problematic. The athlete who idealizes who they are will inevitably devalue themselves after one or two mistakes. The athlete using idealization of the self is unable to realistically view themselves as an admixture of both good and bad attributes. This

DOI: 10.4324/9781003436270-2

defense is commonly seen in American athletes and young athletes, is maladaptive and is the mark of an unsteady and immature sense of identity (Chapter 7).

d Dissociation: This defense is defined as the disruption of memory, consciousness or perception as a way of retaining an illusion of control in the face of extreme stress. This mechanism is commonly referred to as being in the zone, and it is an example of an adaptive defense despite it being labeled as primitive. Tiger Woods would often describe falling into this state when he was in the lead and would say he had no recall of what had happened during the final few holes of play.

e Autistic fantasy: Autistic fantasy is the defense of retreating into a private internal world to avoid anxiety about interpersonal situations. This primitive defense is used by many endurance athletes to good effect. The long hours of isolated practice that is required to get to the top is made easier if the athlete enjoys alone time and can lose themselves in fantasy as they toil away. Ben Hogan is considered one of the greatest ball strikers in golf history and is best characterized as a loner who spent hours on the range digging it out of the dirt. He had an alter ego which he referred to as 'Hennie Bogan.' Pete Sampras was a good example of an athlete who spent long time alone hitting shots against his basement wall as a child and may have also used fantasy to remain focused.

f Thought blocking: Thought blocking is defined as a temporary inhibition of thinking, emotion or behavior and gets little attention in the literature despite the fact that it is an exceedingly common problem. The yips in golf, tennis and baseball pitching, popping jumps in figure skating and freezing in the blocks are all examples of thought blocking.

g Regression: Regression is a return to a previous stage of development or functioning to avoid the anxieties felt in later stages. This is a problem often seen on teams where the structure of a team with coaches and players triggers a regression or pull to childhood behaviors associated with the family structure of parents and siblings. Wilfred Bion's important work in this area (Bion, 1968) will be used to describe regression in an NBA basketball team I worked with in Chapter 12.

h Passive aggression: Passive aggression is seen when an athlete deals with anger by acting nice and smiling but also venting anger indirectly by passive non-compliance. This occurs frequently in younger players who resent being pushed by overly zealous parents or coaches but I've seen this in professional ranks when a team despises a coach and sets about intentionally losing games in order to express their anger and get the coach fired. Chapter 12 describes examples of passive aggression on teams.

i Identification with the aggressor: Introjection involves the taking in of characteristics of a feared other in order to establish a feeling of control.

In Chapter 15, I will outline two cases, one with a boxer and the other with a baseball player to demonstrate the taking in of the character traits of a feared other. Internalizing the traits of an aggressive character can be used to help an athlete inhibit his anxiety or guilt.

j Somatization: This is the tendency to convert psychological feelings into physical symptoms. Somatization is manifest as nausea, vomiting, headaches or back pain. In Chapter 13, I will review a case of a world class soccer star who psychosomatically suffered with migraines, hives and stomach pain.

k Identification with the victim: Identification is a process of internalizing traits from those you admire, but when one identifies with the victim, one feels exaggerated sympathy, empathy and pity, all of which are problematic in competitive sports. I will review examples of athletes with too much empathy, sympathy and pity which prevented them from beating lesser opponents.

The neurotic defenses are as follows:

a Displacement: This defense is used with athletes who hold back frustrations while playing their sport only to take out their frustration on a spouse when they get home. Domestic violence in sports is often due to displacement which highlights the limits of this defense. Displacement is the unconscious shifting of an impulse from one person to another in order to finally express the anger. The case I will review in Chapter 16 involves a star golfer who would systematically take out his frustration on his wife who was exceptionally kind and supportive of him, despite his abuse. Needless to say the use of this defense puts many a marriage in jeopardy.

b Repression: Repression is defined as the expelling or withholding from conscious awareness a feeling or a thought. Chapter 17 will contain the case of an Asian athlete whose ability to repress pain led to a career ending back injury. Repression as defense will also be shown in Chapter 23 in a case involving a well-known PGA golfer who had the ability to repress all feelings of fatigue but which then led to exhaustion, burnout and illness.

c Undoing: Undoing is defined as the attempt to negate a previous action by doing the opposite and is commonly referred to as choking. The familiar "post birdie screw up" in golf is an example of undoing. Chapter 19 will have a case of a golfer who habitually undid his success before he finished the round by choking and giving up the lead.

d Overcompensation: Alfred Adler was responsible for the development of this defense defined as warding off feelings of inferiority by overcompensating through work so that you establish superiority in some domain.

Goertzel and Goertzel's 1962 classic study "Cradles of Eminence" explored the childhood of 300 famous men and women and concluded that the drive to excel derives in part from a sense of inferiority in childhood. Chapter 18 has a case of a world-famous soccer star who grew up in poverty, with no father and who had difficulty processing language. Despite this, she overcompensated and became world renowned.

e Isolation: Isolation can be extremely useful and is defined as the ability to separate emotions from thoughts. I will describe the case of a world class golfer in Chapter 20 who had an astounding ability to isolate his emotions from competitive pressure in major golf tournaments.

f Intellectualization: This is defined as the control of emotions and impulses by excessively thinking about them instead of experiencing them. This enables the athlete to avoid anxiety but as a cost of spontaneity, fluidity, power and grace. Chapter 21 reviews the case of an amateur golfer who was an attorney and how he used an overly intellectual approach to golf and, by so doing, inhibited his club head speed and power.

g Rationalization: Rationalization is defined as the justification of an unacceptable attitude or behavior to avoid feelings of shame or guilt. The case described in Chapter 21 is of a star tennis player who was caught cheating by a television camera but adamantly refused to admit guilt. The failure to admit guilt by rationalizing that he was unaware of what occurred wound up costing him more than $40 million in lost endorsement dollars. The hesitation to admit guilt by using a variety of rationalizations is now considered anathema, and every public relations firm counsels rapid admission of guilt to put the incident behind them.

h Reaction formation: Reaction formation is the transforming of an unacceptable wish or impulse into its opposite. The sports environment requires aggression and dominance, and if one inhibits these traits through reaction formation, it will cost them victory. This defense is ineffective in sports, and it is crucial that the therapist understands this so that more suitable defense can be used. Women who have often been trained to be nice, sweet and smiley, can show signs of reaction formation as do some men who are trained at a young age to always be nice. Chapter 22 describes cases in hockey, soccer and baseball where players had a hard time expressing negative aggressive emotions and how costly that was to them.

The mature defenses are as follows:

a Counterphobias: Counterphobia is based upon a childhood fear but rather than fleeing the source of the fear, it is sought out in order to overcome it. Freud suggested that thrill-seeking behaviors, including sports, are counterphobic in nature. When an athlete seeks out the challenge of competition, they may be unconsciously trying to prove that they are strong and not weak. Chapter 24 will have a description of a professional golfer who constantly provoked controversial situations in order to overcome his original fears he faced in childhood at the hands of a violent and threatening father.

b   Self-observation: Self-observation is the ability to reflect upon one's own feelings and behaviors without distortion, grandiosity or self-attack. It can be considered the sine qua non of mental health. The obtaining of this mature defense is a significant achievement and is elaborated in Chapter 25 with two cases, one of an amateur golfer who was able to pause and gather himself when experiencing tournament pressure. The other was of an ex college pitcher who learned how to let minor incidents fall away without taking them personally.

c   Altruism and altruistic surrender: Altruism is seen by fulfilling the needs of others and by so doing obtaining some level of gratification and pride. This is the defining characteristic of a good team player and every coaches' dream. The altruistic athlete is non-envious, supportive of teammates and is well-liked. However, too much altruism in sports is tantamount to what Anna Freud (1966) would call altruistic surrender or masochism and what Donald Winnicott (1971) referred to as the false self. Great athletes must have a balance of altruism and self-centeredness. We will review a case of an All-American rugby player who was exceptionally altruistic and which benefited her team but not necessarily herself.

d   Anticipation: Anticipation is the ability to plan ahead, prepare, worry and get ready for future discomfort. This is often referred to as Murphy's Law which was first developed by a mountaineer who realized that when climbing a mountain all problematic contingencies must be planned for or the hike could end in death. All athletes must be able to anticipate and be prepared for all contingencies, occurrences and problems, and this is one of the most useful aspects of standard cognitive behavioral sport psychology. In Chapter 27, I will review a case which shows the proper anticipation in golf.

e   Asceticism: Asceticism is the renunciation of pleasurable aspects of an experience. This mechanism can be used in the service of spiritual or athletic goals. The well-known effort to remain celibate prior to a boxing match to enhance performance was demonstrated in the film classic "Raging Bull" where Jake LaMotta was able to withstand the charms of his beautiful wife for two weeks prior to a championship fight. Asceticism by renouncing rest, sleep, food or sex in order to practice more is used by many serious athletes. The case shown in Chapter 28 is about a world class professional lacrosse player who adhered to a schedule of five hours sleep per night and endless hours of grueling workouts in order to get to the top in his field.

f Humor: Humor is the ability to find comic or ironic elements in difficult situations to reduce unpleasant emotions. Humor is a highly valued defense and explains why comics like Adam Sandler and Jim Carrey command some of the largest salaries in the film industry. Dr. Mark Nesti of the English Premier League has observed that banter in the locker room is crucial for tension relief and characterizes the tone of many winning teams (Nesti, 2010). Chapter 29 contains three jokes told to me by athletes as examples of the use of humor used to cope with dreadful situations.

g Suppression: Suppression is the ability to temporarily avoid thinking about a disturbing problem or an upcoming occurrence. This is a valuable skill for athletes since it means they're able to 'stay in the moment,' that tough to find place where focus is maintained and fantasies of winning or losing are avoided. Chapter 30 explores the amazing ability of Asian women on the Ladies Professional Golf Association to use suppression to remain poised coming down the stretch.

h Sublimation: Sublimation is the channeling of aggressive or sexual impulses into socially acceptable forms. Sports requires the channeling of aggression into something socially valued. Sublimation allows for aggression, anger and hostility to be expressed but with social valence and usefulness. Nearly every athlete needs to tap into their aggression to win, and if they sublimate rather than repress, act out or regress, they will perform much better. In Chapter 31, I will discuss two cases of young men who had much rage and needed help in channeling it correctly. In Chapter 32, I discuss the way sexuality is also involved in sports and how I helped a beautiful young tennis star deal with the leers and lechery of male fans.

References

Bion, W. (1968) *Experiences in Groups*. Routledge.
Freud, A. (1966) *The Ego and the Mechanisms of Defense*. International Universities Press.
Nesti, M. (2010) *Psychology in Football: Working with Elite and Professional Players*. Routledge.
Vaillant, G. (1992) *Ego Mechanisms of Defense: A Guide for Clinicians and Researchers*. American Psychiatric Press.
Winnicott, D.W. (1971) *Playing and Reality*. Routledge.

2 Why Defense Mechanisms Must Be Addressed Prior to Teaching Coping Skills?

There are many differences between defense mechanisms and coping skills. Coping skills are cognitive behavioral techniques ostensibly designed to help the athlete cope with competitive stress. These well-known mental game tools include goal-setting, relaxation strategies, deep breathing, meditation, positive self-talk, rational emotive therapy (RET), assertiveness training and visualization, and they make up the backbone of the standard sport psychology practice (Murphy, 1996). Defense mechanisms serve the same purpose of anxiety management. The difference is that the defenses are developed by the athlete in childhood and are their way of coping with stress. These include repression, denial, rationalization, suppression, acting out, intellectualization, dissociation, humor, asceticism, sublimation and more, and they are part of the focus in a standard psychoanalytic practice.

Which method of handling stress is better for the athlete, learning new coping skills or using naturally occurring defenses? Can you do both? Do these two processes conflict with each other? I believe that adaptive coping skills cannot and will not be used by the athlete until they have achieved a certain level of ego strength. Prior to this, the athlete will employ primitive or neurotic defense mechanisms to protect themselves from growth, learning or success since they are not fully equipped to deal with success. The athlete must assimilate insights and develop ego strength in order to finally accommodate to new coping skills.

Norma Hann's book "Coping and Defending" (1977) comes closest to addressing the differences between defenses and coping skills, and her work is based upon Piaget's cognitive developmental theory of assimilation and accommodation. She suggests that defenses tend to be primitive and often repress or inhibit success whereas coping skills are more mature. She feels people must be helped to develop ego strength in order to assimilate and use coping skills tools. This idea that athletes' ego must first be strengthened prior to the learning of coping skills makes sense.

It is common knowledge that athletes resist sport psychology for a host of reasons. It is possible that part of their resistance is because the coping skills being taught are in conflict with previously established defenses (Ferraro & Rush, 2002). It may be that many of the behavioral coping skills don't sink in because the athlete is already using their own instinctive, overlearned, unconscious methods of coping. Their defenses are entrenched into the athlete's perceptual apparatus and they are taking place outside of awareness. Let us define terms.

DEFENSE MECHANISMS: Defense mechanisms are naturally occurring processes similar to biological processes and provide solutions to human anxiety and stress. Many of the defenses including denial, repression, acting, sublimation, anticipation, humor and asceticism are fairly effective coping methods. Freud was the first to describe defense mechanisms, and since then, Anna Freud (1966), George Vaillant (1992) and Phebe Cramer (2006) have made major contributions to the field. Defenses are mankind's way of repressing internal and external stress and are compromise positions which help the athlete cope but sometimes at a cost of energy and power.

COPING SKILLS: Lazarus is acknowledged as one of the first major researchers on stress and coping skills (Lazarus & Folkman, 1984). He suggested that internal stress reactions were based upon ones appraisal of the external stimulus. If it was deemed dangerous, one would feel stress, and this reaction would also be contingent upon one's sense of confidence or effectiveness. He investigated the causes of psychological breakdowns in military settings, concentration camps and breakdowns due to traumatic injury. He coined the phrase eustress, differentiating it from distress and emphasized how the appraisal of a setting influences how one reacted to it. His theories of stress and coping have been used by the behavior modifiers who came after him, including Leonard Krasner (1995) and Albert Ellis (Ellis and Maclaren, 2005). This coping skills approach has a commonsense appeal to it but always there is an urgency for quick solutions to difficult problems.

I recall a conversation I had with Bob Rotella, one of golf's foremost sport psychologists. As I discussed his approach to working on the PGA, he casually remarked to me that if you don't show results very quickly, you're gone. This is a telling comment and helps explain the anxious compulsive nature of the field of sport psychology today. His remark also reveals the weakness in the field. Short-term interventions to change panic attacks, the yips or major slumps are destined to fail. I believe that for any intervention to take hold inside the athlete, it must contain two elements, one of which is largely unconscious. As an example, let's take an athlete who is overly harsh and self-critical. I believe that the following two-step process must unfold.

1) If this athlete is harsh on himself, the intervention must be somewhat psychoeducational by suggesting one try to be more forgiving. If a player

has anger issues, the therapist needs to mirror back "Oh, I see you're very negative, it would be wise to try to be more forgiving." This approach is, matter of fact, practical and characterizes the standard sport psychology approach. However, merely to repeat this commonsense approach each time the player gets angry quickly wears thin and becomes vacuous and then meaningless. This standard psychoeducational approach is to teach, instruct, model, implore, demand, suggest, cajole, reinforce and repeat to the athlete rational positive self-talk and try to be less harsh and more forgiving. However, to do this is to quickly come to the realization that you're hitting your head against a wall. A better way to put this is that you are hitting your head against the athlete's defense mechanisms.

2) Therefore, prior to or along side the above coping skill approach, the intervention must offer insight into the genesis of the athlete's self-attack. Harshness is often learned from a parent or a coach. Revealing the connection between a present attitude and from whence it came helps the athlete to accept the intervention as valid and interesting. This is the process of insight or that 'aha' moment. Even then, insight is not enough because the defenses will work to push the insight out of awareness. Insights invariably are repressed which means that the therapist must retain a memory of this insight and use it again and again as new forms of self-attack emerge. Behavior therapy has attempted to overcome this kind of resistance by assigning homework to the athlete but this has little impact. One must patiently await the next example of harshness to emerge. When this occurs enough, one will slowly see a change. This is called the working through process and there is nothing quick about it. I believe any effective sport psychology must have the commonsense face validity of the coping skill approach, but it must connect to the athlete's past and insights must be worked through over and over again. There is no rushing this (Kahn, 1989).

> The coping mechanisms of standard sport psychology such as goal-setting, relaxation therapy, positive self-talk, rational emotive therapy, autogenics, meditation, visualization and acceptance therapy definitely parallel the more adaptive defense mechanisms. Goal-setting mirrors the defense mechanism of anticipation. Relaxation therapy to control the athlete's anxiety parallels the defenses of suppression and repression which expels from consciousness unwanted feelings like anxiety. Positive self-talk and rational emotive therapy are standard coping techniques to help the athlete to reason away high levels of anxiety. These tools parallel rationalization and intellectualization, the defense mechanisms which use rational thinking to cope with upsetting emotions or circumstances.

Defense Mechanisms and Teaching Coping Skills 15

An understanding of the deeper levels of the mind is the key to change. No matter how well one applies coping skills, an understanding of the underlying defenses, the athlete's resistance to change, unconscious fixations and the development of ego strength are needed if one hopes to see the athlete change either on or off the playing field. Exploring defenses and underlying problems is a necessary key in order to apply coping skills that adhere.

Key Points

- Little has been written about the differences between the cognitive-behavior therapy coping skills and defense mechanisms, and how they compliment or contradict each other.
- Defense mechanisms are unconscious internal processes all athletes use to cope with stress. Some are more effective than others.
- Coping skills are consciously applied ways to manage emotional stress during competition.
- It may be that athletes fail to use coping skills because they may be in conflict with their natural defense mechanisms.
- The mature defenses are similar to some of the coping skills being taught by sport psychologists.
- In the future, there will come a time that coping skills and defenses are integrated.

Reflective Questions

- How would you define a defense mechanism?
- What is the difference between a defense mechanism and a coping skill?
- Can you name one defense mechanism that you use every day?
- What is the most effective coping skill you've ever used?

Exercises for Best Performance

Exercise #1: Practice using humor either in the locker room or on the playing field at least once per game.

> **Tips for Best Performance**
>
> The most mature defenses include humor, suppression, anticipation and self-observation. This text will outline these defenses and talk about how to develop them.

Exercise #2: To stay in the moment, one must learn to suppress thoughts. A good practice drill is to train oneself to not look at the clock when going somewhere and simply concentrate on the road. Golfers should train themselves to not look at scoreboards and not look at opponents when they are swinging.

References

Cramer, P. (2006) *Protecting the Self: Defense Mechanisms in Action*. The Guilford Press.

Ellis, A. & MacLaren, K. (2005) *Rational Emotive Therapy; A Therapists Guide*. Impact Publishing.

Ferraro, T. & Rush, S. (2002) Why Athletes Resist Sport Psychology. *Athletic Insight*, 2(3).pp. 10–16.

Freud, A. (1966) *The Ego and the Mechanisms of Defense*. International Universities Press.

Haan, N. (1997) *Coping and Defending; Processes of Self-Environment Organization*. Academic Press.

Kahn, M. (1989) *The Loing Wait and Other Psychoanalytic Narratives*. Summit Books.

Krasner, L. (1995) *Theories in Behavior Therapy: Philosophical and Historical Contexts. In Theories of Behavior Therapy: Exploring Behavior Change* (eds. W. O'Donohue & L. Krasner). American Psychological Association.

Lazarus, R. & Folkman, S. (1984) *Stress Appraisal and Coping*. Springer Publishing.

Murphy, S. (1996) *The Achievement Zone: 8 Skills for Winning All the Time from the Playing Field to the Boardroom*. G.P. Putnam's Sons.

Vaillant, G. (1992) *Ego Mechanisms of Defense: A Guide for Clinicians and Researchers*. American Psychiatric Press.

3 Emotional Breakdowns in Athletes

Why They Happen and What to Do About Them

At age 23, the Japanese professional tennis star Naomi Osaka was the highest paid female athlete in the world and suddenly quit tennis. After refusing to speak to the press following her Sunday first round match, she was promptly fined $15,000 by the French Federation of Tennis. In response to this, she withdrew stating "The truth is that I have suffered long bouts of depression since the US Open in 2018 and I have had a really hard time coping with that." Not only was this a huge loss to tennis fans throughout the world, but it also highlights the level of stress and mental anguish all professional athletes face. Naomi Osaka expressed herself honestly during her mental breakdown when she said "I'm a shy private person and have a lot of anxiety when I talk to the press."

This is not the first high-profile athlete to have a public breakdown. The American Simone Biles, the best gymnast in history and five-time Olympic medalist suddenly withdrew from the team and individual all-around competitions at the 2020 Tokyo Olympics. She left the finals after struggling to land her vault and later said she was prioritizing her mental health and withdrew from further competition.

How best to understand these breakdowns? A breakdown of defenses can be explained by referring to the literature on trauma. Lenore Terr (1999), a leading theorist on trauma, defines trauma as a sudden external blow or series of blows which renders one temporarily helpless by breaking past ordinary defensive operations. Once this trauma occurs, a number of lasting changes seem to take place, including a loss of a sense of safety, sleep issues, startle responses, developmental regression, avoidance behaviors, irritability and hypervigilance. Trauma means that the person no longer feels safe in the world, no longer feels confident. Young athletes with undeveloped defenses and who are exposed to fame are susceptible to breakdowns of defense. Sports are played in front of others, sometimes many others, and when loss occurs, this is embarrassing and it can be shattering. Like the children's poem of Humpty Dumpty who had a great fall and couldn't be put back together again, when a young star falls from grace, the loss can shatter the defenses which had previously provided a sense of safety and confidence.

Thousands of adoring fans, huge amounts of money, millions watching on TV, screaming coaches make high-level sports one of the most stressful environments there is.

Talent is like a horse and the athlete is its rider. And if the athlete is too young, it can be very difficult to manage the talent. And fame is often a poisoned chalice which is glamorous at first but soon turns toxic. Sports can produce injury but it can also produce mental breakdowns, especially for the younger elite athlete who has not developed strong enough defenses to manage stress. How is a young athlete supposed to handle TV cameras and post-game interviews? I recall watching one of my athletes being interviewed on TV immediately following a nationally televised race which she won. She seemed to handle the interview well, but when I saw her face to face in our next session, she told me as soon as the interview ended, she vomited on the ground.

When the defenses begin to break down, the athlete develops symptoms such as the yips, heart palpitations, tremors, nausea and bizarre thoughts. If these symptoms are not treated properly, this turns into depression and can end a career. This is what the world witnessed with Naomi Osaka and Simone Biles.

I will present a number of cases of famous athletes I have treated who have suffered breakdowns.

Case #1: This is the case of a 25-year-old PGA golfer who first showed signs of the breakdown of defenses during the British Open as he was vying for the lead on Saturday's third round. He was two shots off the pace, and on the 14th hole, he removed a twig near his ball in the rough before he hit his shot. After he hit the shot, he began to ruminate that maybe the ball moved as he removed the twig which would have meant a penalty. He conferred with an official who reassured him that it was not an infraction since he was still uncertain as to whether the ball moved. Despite this reassurance, the stress of being near the lead and the guilt over this possible infraction continued to obsess him over the next six months. He then began to obsessively modify the way he marked his ball, worry about whether he touched the ball with his putter, etc. This obsessive-compulsive behavior and this guilt reflected the emergence anxiety and a sign that his formerly strong defenses were breaking down. He began to hesitate and flinch while hitting shots, his game weakened, confidence eroded and he lost his playing privileges. Therapy with this player entailed helping him to regain confidence by exploring the underlying conflicts of guilt about making more money than his siblings, his parents and peers. This case highlights the way chronic competitive stress weakens defenses and how a minor incident can be the straw that breaks the camel's back. When this occurs, the athlete reverts to lower levels of defense to manage the anxiety. In this case, the lower-level defenses included intellectualization, overthinking and self-doubt.

Case #2: This 25-year-old professional baseball player first showed signs of defense breakdown when he was 14 years of age. He had gained national recognition as a young player and was ranked #1 in the nation for his age. He received local press attention and was scouted by Major League Baseball. He was invited into more than one bit league team locker room. As this unfolded, he began to have performance problems both at the plate and on the field. He became hesitant and stiff. He began to experience numbness in the hands and arms while batting. Simultaneously, his father, who was also experiencing national attention for the first time began to overuse cocaine and was arrested. Due to his considerable talent as a young ball player, he managed to continue to play at a high level and eventually received a full scholarship to play in a Division I college. However, his defenses had shattered and broken down at age 14 and this trauma had never healed. He continuously felt panic and numbness in the hands and hesitation on the field at third base. He made it to AA pro ball but lingered there. He no longer was able to remain focused and lost his ability to ignore crowds. It is no surprise that a 14-year-old with immature defenses would break down under this kind of attention, praise and fame. We worked hard to establish insight, but in this case, the athlete had already grown dependent on drugs as a defense. We now were faced with trying to help him reduce drug intake and also understand the initial time of the breakdown nine years prior.

Case #3: This is a case of a tennis player who was able to maintain an overidealized defense throughout his teens with the help of parental praise and media attention. However, he was awarded a college scholarship to one of the great tennis colleges in America and was faced with teammates who were every bit as good as he. At this point, his grandiose overidealized defense was no longer tenable as he failed to break into the top five spots on the college's travel team. His overidealized defense shattered within the first year of play. He began to devalue himself, feel self-doubt, anxiety, shame and depression. This in turn led to his coach giving him a series of confusing lessons which only worsened matters. His college career was abysmal, and upon graduating, he watched as his teammates went on to gain fame and stardom on the tennis circuit. He went home, became a teaching pro and then regained his amateur standing, continuing to play competitive events but was still filled with doubt, anxiety and shame. He arrived in my office when he was about 50 years old: having had an unfilled professional and amateur career in a sport he had tremendous talent in. Basic efforts to instill standard coping skills such as deep breathing relaxation therapy and visualization to manage anxiety were of little use. We then worked on insight into when he first experienced his defensive breakdown which meant we revisited his college experience. Throughout this work, we also made efforts to understand his previous use of an overidealized defense and attempted to create more mature defenses, including self-observation, suppression, sublimation, affiliation and humor.

Case #4: Dan was a very talented 21-year-old quarterback football player recruited to play at an Ivy League college. It was expected that he would be a starter as a freshman and he performed well that year. However, during his sophomore year, he incurred a slight injury and was sidelined for two weeks where upon he began to ruminate about what he called "the worst possible outcome" which was to be permanently benched and replaced by a substitute. There was no evidence that this was about to happen, but nonetheless, this rumination became entrenched, and when he returned to play after his recovery, his play was characterized as hesitation, self-doubting and stiff. He was eventually sidelined and benched permanently. This led to him calling me. During intake, he repeatedly used the phrase 'the worst possible outcome' when describing his habit of catastrophizing. I noted this to him and asked him to talk more about the repeated use of this term. He freely associated with his first real loss in life when his childhood football coach suddenly died of a heart attack. The patient was ten years old at the time. Following that sudden and unexpected loss, he began to compulsively worry that his parents would die when they were out of the house and he would call to see if they were alright. This was 'the worst possible outcome' of any separation from him. I hypothesized that the initial traumatic loss of his coach was unresolved, shattered his childhood feeling of safety and confidence. He compensated for this loss and was able to cope with the variety of small losses as he played football, but his fear of 'the worst possible outcome' eventually re-emerged when he was benched due to his injury during his sophomore year in college. The temporary removal from the playing field was sufficiently similar to the permanent loss due to the death of his childhood coach that all the past emotions, memories, sadness and fears came flooding back and broke through his defenses. As these emotions flooded him, he lost form, lost confidence and was benched. His college coach would not have the time nor the ability to help him with any of this, and neither would standard here-and-now interventions that ignored his past trauma.

There are many ways to deal with the traumatic breakdowns suffered by athletes. Their breakdowns often go untreated or are inadequately treated. Every case is different. Sometimes, a minor loss in the present will cause a breakdown because it opens up deeper unresolved loses experienced in childhood. Sometimes, a young superstar implodes under the pressure of fame. Sometimes, an athlete is overworked, has failed to rest properly and this depletion weakens the defenses and a breakdown follows. One must attune oneself to their experience, empathize and solace as the athlete shares their painful stories. This often elicits tears, a sign that affect is being felt and resolved. This must be accompanied by a discussion of the athlete's evident ability and former style of confident play. Insight into the actual causes of the current collapse along with ego support and solace is needed for the athlete to regain confidence.

Reflective Questions

- What causes an athlete to have a breakdown?
- Why do you think younger players often have breakdowns?
- Why does fame produce so much stress?

Exercise Drills for Best Performance

- Exercise #1: Get into the habit of protecting your energy by taking naps when you want to.
- Exercise #2: Make sure you get to bed early enough to guarantee eight hours of sleep each night. If you must rise by 6 AM, you need to be in bed by 10 PM.
- Exercise #3: It is wise to become aware of symptoms of irritability. These are warning signs that your defenses are weakening. If you realize you are constantly irritable, find a trusted adviser who listens well and discuss your concerns at length. Do not be afraid to ventilate feelings to them.

Reflective Questions

- Defenses usually function well, but competitive stress is chronic and unrelenting the defenses will breakdown and emotions will spill forth.
- Breakdowns occur when the defenses are not fully matured and the athlete has not been able to find better defense to cope with their stress.
- Breakdowns frequently occur when an athlete reaches a new level of rank or status and they have not had the time to accommodate to a new lifestyle.
- The athlete will need support to gain an understanding of what happened to them and how to develop better defenses or coping skills.

> Tips for Best Performance
>
> It is wise to become aware of symptoms of anxiety or fatigue. These are warning signs that your defenses are weakening. Find a trusted adviser who listens well and discuss your concerns at length.

Recommended Viewing

- The Netflix docuseries about Naomi Osaka directed by Garrett Bradley displays the toll that fame had on the young star.
- King Richard, the 2021 biographical sports drama starring Will Smith who plays Richard Williams, the protective father of the Williams sisters and how he managed to shield them from fame until they were ready for it.

Reference

Terr, L. (1999) Childhood Traumas: An Outline and Overview. In *Essential Papers on Posttraumatic Stress Disorder* (Ed. M. Horowitz). New York University Press, 61–81.

Part 1
Immature Defenses

Meglio e la piccolo certezza che la gran bugia
(the little truth is better than the big lie) – Leonardo da Vinci

Immature defenses are thought of as the simplest form of defense and they're commonplace in sports. Athletes can overuse and get fixated on primitive defenses because of early childhood loss, illness, neglect or abuse. This section will contain a discussion of the variety of immature and maladaptive defenses including denial, drug use, grandiosity, depersonalization, autistic fantasy, perfectionism, superstitions, regression, somatization and more.

4 Denial Mechanisms in an Aging Athlete

Denial is a primitive defense defined as a process whereby external reality is denied. One sees or hears things but refuses to acknowledge what is seen or heard. Denial means one is avoiding the awareness of some painful aspect of reality. As an example, when a patient is told he has terminal cancer and responds to the news by saying "Thanks Doc, I'm glad that all is well," this is considered denial. Along these lines, the Swiss-American psychiatrist Elizabeth Kubler-Ross found that denial was the first of the five stages a patient went through as they approached their death (1969). Sigmund Freud characterized denial as psychotic (1924), but since then, denial has been described as a more common though primitive defense.

The defense of denial is commonplace in sports. NASCAR drivers who push speed are actively employing denial to keep out of awareness just how close they are to death. When Dale Earnhardt was killed, the NASCAR circuit did not pause for a moment. The race must go on. Ernest Becker's book "Denial of Death" (1973) suggested that mankind has established elaborate denial mechanisms to shield ourselves from this grim reality that we all die someday. The religious belief in an afterlife is another example of denial (Freud, 1923).

Denial is commonly seen in middle age or elderly athletes as a defense against the awareness that they are aging and slowly weakening. The result is that many athletes hold onto their careers well beyond reason. Mohammed Ali boxed longer than he should have and thus incurred brain damage and Parkinson's diseases.

The case I will explore here is a 76-year-old amateur tennis player who was in denial about aging and felt he should still play competitively against younger men despite his age. He had once competed at the national level but was well beyond that stage of performance. Yet, he seemed to deny his age and pouted and became angry whenever he played. When he called me, he explained that he needed some kind of help but was unsure what. He told me he was about to quit tennis because he was so angry with himself.

During our work together, his demeanor was at first guarded and aloof, the stereotype of an entitled upper-class person whose wealth has sheltered him from the harsh realities of life. However, time is not to be denied and his inability to deal with aging had produced a narcissistic crisis for him. I had to help him to grasp the narcissistic crisis that aging had caused and the anger and shame he felt as he experienced the inevitable slowing of physical ability. When I first met him, he used anger and alcohol to deny this reality, the reality that he had a 76-year-old body. I began the work with acknowledgment, admiration and mirroring of his previous talents so that he would be equipped to handle the shame of aging without collapsing into despair. This helped him to temporarily shore up his shame, and in addition, I provided him with standard cognitive positive self-talk tips as well as encouraging him to use joking and humor following any missed shots at the net or with his serve as another way to deal with shame.

> The issue of outstaying ones welcome in sports is rarely seen in the case of South Korean women who play professional golf on the LPGA. I recall that during a book tour years ago through Seoul, I spoke with a group of journalists who worried that they had no Julie Inksters in South Korea, golfers who played late into their careers. Instead, what they saw was that female players from South Korea would make a big splash on the LPGA and within a few years return home to marry and have children. This meant that fans were not able to establish a connection with them.

Narcissists need attunement and positive mirroring to help them overcome loss and disappointments, and with sufficient attunement, the ego strength of the athlete will rise and he or she will be in a better position to deal with the losses (Kohut, 1977). This strategy worked well enough in this case as the tennis player's demeanor warmed. Unfortunately, and as is often the case, this was a short-term case which lasted over only three weekends where I went to his club to work with him.

After the attunement phase, I would have introduced some logotherapy to help this athlete to find other ways to add meaning to his life outside of competitive tennis (Frankl, 1959). The search for meaning after one's competitive years are over is a crucial and difficult task, given the sense of power and excitement provided by success in the competitive sports arena. Little can compare to the applause the athlete feels as he or she lifts a trophy, gets press coverage and gets a taste of fame. Logotherapy is an existential approach to patients, established by Viktor Frankl, the psychiatrist who survived two years in Auschwitz and then wrote the book

26 Immature Defenses

"Man's Search for Meaning." This book is considered a classic in the field of psychoanalysis by extending therapeutic focus beyond issues of pleasure and power into the more spiritual concerns of transcendence and finding

> A glimpse into the defense of denial can be had by viewing the 1990 Italian film "Everybody's Fine" directed by Giuseppe Tornatore and starring Marcello Mastroianni as an aging bureaucrat who visits his five grown children who live in various parts of Italy. The film does a good job of showing his denial of the reality of their lives, as he endeavors to pretend that they are all happy and successful.

true meaning in life. However, we never had a chance to enter this second phase of the work since he prematurely terminated.

To summarize, denial is a common and primitive defense often seen in aging athletes who refuse to leave the field of play and move aside, to make room for younger athletes who are on the rise. Denial can produce anger, injury, a failure to grow and cause inappropriate use of prescription or illegal drugs which can give temporary energy to the aging body. Treatment usually entails first identifying the defense of denial and then mirror the athletes talents and accomplishments. This can lead to helping them to replace denial with more mature defenses such as altruism, humor or sublimation.

Key Points

- Denial is considered a primitive defense defined as avoiding the awareness of some painful aspect of reality.
- The aging or the injured athlete will often engage in denial to avoid the awareness that their body can no longer function as it once did.
- It is helpful to consistently acknowledge and mirror the aging athlete's former power and accomplishments in order to shore up damaged self-esteem.
- The use of logotherapy or helping the athlete to find new purpose for their life. One can become an ambassador for one's sport rather than a competitor.

Reflective Questions

- How would you define the defense of denial?
- Are race car drivers, jockeys and cliff divers in denial of death? Explain.

- Why is denial considered to be such a primitive, ineffective and maladaptive defense?
- What is the best way to help an older athlete in denial about his or her age?

Tips for Best Performance

As performance declines over time, one ought to employ humor and self-talk which can provide solace. In addition, it is crucial to find meaning and purpose outside of performance on the playing field.

Exercise Drills for Best Performance

- If you find yourself getting too angry over minor mistakes, you may be in denial about your human fallibility. To overcome this state of denial, it will be necessary to learn forgiveness and self-acceptance. After any mistake, get into the habit of saying to yourself, "I'm only human and to be human is good enough."
- During aging, the athlete's performance declines. Rather than being in denial of this cruel fact of life, get into the habit of using humor and joking aloud so that you ventilate your disappointment and transcend it with humor.
- As the athlete ages and the satisfactions of physical excellence diminish, it is wise to develop more sedentary and cerebral hobbies in order to maintain self-esteem, joy and meaning in life. This is called sublimation and is a mature and adaptive defense.

Recommended Reading

Viktor Frankl's "Man's Search for Meaning" by Beacon Press.

Recommending Viewing

The 1990 Italian film "Everybody's Fine" directed by Giuseppe Tornatore and starring Marcello Mastroianni (not the 2009 American version or the 2016 Chinese version).

References

Becker, E. (1973) *The Denial of Death*. Simon and Schuster.
Frankl, V. (1959) *Mans' Search for Meaning*. Beacon Press.
Freud, S. (1923) *The Ego and The Id Standard Edition*. W.W. Norton & Company, 19, 13–59.
Kohut, H. (1977) *The Restoration of the Self*. International Universities Press.
Kubler-Ross, E. (1969) *On Death and Dying*. Routledge.

5 Acting Out, Impulsivity and Drug Use in Athletes

Acting out is an immature defense defined as an impulsive action taken to avoid mounting pain, fatigue, anxiety or pressure. Many athletes act out by rushing shots or by taking drugs to avoid the pain of competitive pressure. The athlete faces anxiety, tension, pain and fatigue on a daily basis, and these emotional states can be very difficult to manage. Most athletes rationalize drug use by saying it helps to improve performance, but the truth is that drugs can alleviate anxiety but hurts performance. In this chapter, we will discuss how a golfer used drugs and a tennis player used hasty high-risk shots to get away from the tension of the moment. Stress, mounting fatigue or impatience can induce athletes to act and impulsive action can produce unforced errors to end the stress.

Freud (1911–1913) realized drug use was a method of coping with pain, and he was one of the first researchers to explore how cocaine could be used as a pain suppressor. His daughter, Anna Freud (1966) suggested that drugs were frequently used as a defense against anxiety, deprivation or frustration. Wurmser's classic text, "The Hidden Dimension: Psychodynamics in Compulsive Drug Use" is an extensive psychoanalytic study of drug use, and he describes drug use as a "direct pharmacogenic affect defense with the drug user seeking the solution to an inner problem on the outside, in action and in concrete form." (1978, p. 146). A variety of emotions are warded off by the ingestion of a substance. One of the many problems with compulsive drug use is that it prevents the athlete from internalizing their own value, power, self-reliance and self-esteem.

Athletes are drawn to drugs to magically supply themselves with self-esteem and power, but outside of small doses of caffeine, there is no proof that the use of any drug enhances performance (Wadler & Hainline, 1989). The steroid scandal in Major League Baseball is one example of drug use in sports, and headlines constantly report how athletes test positive to some illegal drugs.

> The Irish and alcohol use. The Irish are good-humored, charming and hospitable without being intimate. They are seen as jokesters; however, they seem to struggle against loneliness (McGoldrick, 1997). As Roberts & Myers (1954) put it, the damp climate, the cold, being stuck indoors and the grief of all this has prompted this clan to use alcohol as a single form of escape. It is not unusual to observe Irish golfers on tour pick up a pint and kick back and enjoy life. This group is a good example of a group using the defense of acting out in order to avoid pain, sadness and anxiety.

CASE STUDY #1: This 28-year-old tennis player used both prescribed and illegal drugs to manage his fatigue and anxiety. As a child, he was a talented soccer player, but he matured slowly, and since he was small, he was bullied both on the soccer field and in class. His anxiety became so great that he was sent to a psychiatrist and was prescribed both antidepressants and tranquilizers. His parents and the psychiatrist all encouraged his use of medication rather than teaching other ways of managing this stress. He gave up soccer at that point and took up tennis. Over time, he grew physically and psychologically to become a young man who was tall, good looking, intelligent, with social grace, refined etiquette. He began to play tennis more competitively at this point and began to harbor fantasies of making it onto the tennis circuit. He was tall, strong and smart and he did well in tennis. He had excellent coaches and he began to enter national-level tournaments. With this, his anxiety grew and he began to use marijuana and alcohol to manage his anxiety while playing. He had never learned more mature defenses given his early use of prescribed drugs to manage stress.

My patient's underlying unconscious motivation in playing tennis competitively was to face his childhood fears and to defeat the bullies of his past. This motivational pattern was well described by Freud in his essay "Repeating, Remembering and Working Through" (1914) where individuals became compelled to enter the arena they were most afraid of. This compulsion, which my patient had, only worsened his anxiety and thus it was predictable that he would turn to drug use to control the anxiety. The taking of drugs can now be seen for what it was, an immature acting out in order to avoid the anxiety felt during competition.

We slowly came to realize that his use of marijuana and alcohol was an impulsive avoidance of overwhelming anxiety stemming from early childhood experience of being bullied. Using marijuana and alcohol was an action or an acting out to find an external answer to an inner unconscious problem. Only after his history was explored and insight was gained over a two-year twice weekly process, did he find a way to stop taking marijuana and stop drinking. We first focused on the feelings that the marijuana and alcohol were providing him with. They helped him to avoid competitive anxiety and to also avoid feelings of weakness by replacing this affect with a feeling of power and strength. However, the loss of focus, dehydration and lethargy the drugs produced in him undid any of the supposed benefits.

Following this insight, we discussed ways to accept and tolerate the inevitable effects of excitement and anxiety experienced during play. In addition, it becomes necessary to help the patient establish a new more competitive identity prior to matches. When trying to help an athlete to establish a stronger identity after insight is gained, I usually use George Kelly's Personal Construct Theory (Kelly, 1992). Kelly's is like a 'fake it till you make it' intervention where you teach the athlete to accommodate to a new identity as he sheds his old acting out defense.

Overtime, the insights gained allowed him to understand that the trauma of being bullied in childhood produced a weak and fragile ego which was why he needed marijuana and alcohol to cover up this anxiety and weakness. This awareness allowed him to establish a more focused and aggressive attitude while playing tennis, and he went on to become a serious amateur tennis player with no need to resort to drugs to maintain power. The insights gained in analysis helped him to give up his primitive acting out defense of marijuana use, alcohol use and replaced them with more mature defenses such as self-observation, identification with the aggressor and humor. The treatment has not been quick and it has not been easy, but to use the patient's own assessment, it has been lifesaving.

BRIEF CASE STUDY OF A TENNIS PLAYER WHO ACTED OUT BY TAKING RISKY SHOTS TO AVOID THE TENSION OF LONG POINTS: Acting out is defined as an impulsive action designed to avoid painful effects. Drug use is not the only way that acting out occurs. This is the case of a 19-year-old male tennis player who could not tolerate the tension felt as a point was prolonged with baseline shots. Instead, he took action or "acted out" by taking risky low-percentage shots in order to remove himself from the heightening tension felt during long rallies. I believe the use of this acting out defense in tennis is common. Rather than patiently wait for an opening, he would rush the net, over hit or take a risky shot to get himself away from the tension. This was a highly ranked national-level player who had a team of handlers who had already invested significant time and money to further his career, and he seemed resistant to changing this strategy no matter how many times the coach implored him to do so. This problem was resolved with insight into the defense he was using unconsciously. I had been working with him for more than a year before this acting out error began to emerge. As he improved, he faced stronger players who could extend rallies. His acting out tennis strategy to

32   Immature Defenses

finish points off quickly was not working. He had great difficulty coping with anxiety felt during longer rallies. We had a good working alliance and he was open to interpretations. He began to adopt a more patient, less impulsive strategy of play and so he made fewer and fewer unforced errors.

Key Points

- Acting out refers to a defense where impulsive action is taken to avoid anxiety or fatigue.
- Drug use can be seen as acting out to avoid anxiety during competition; however, during drug intake will often has numerous negative side effects, including loss of focus and loss of energy.
- Impulsive shot making in tennis can be seen as an acting out to avoid mounting tension and to get the point over as quickly as possible. This common problem usually leads to losses.

Reflective Questions

- What is the definition of the defense called "acting out" and explain why it is considered maladaptive?
- Drug intake is a form of acting out defenses. Why is drug use so frequent in sports?
- Why do some athletes have so much trouble with the concept of patience and how is impatience such a big problem in sports?

Tips for Best Performance

If you notice that you are taking drugs too often, it may be because you are trying to avoid competitive anxiety. Find someone to help you to explore why you think you need the drug. You will quickly learn that talking helps and it never has nasty side effects either.

Exercise Drills for Best Performance

- If you notice that you are drinking excessive alcohol, or taking drugs too often, during competition, you may be trying to cope with competitive anxiety. A better way to manage anxiety is to use self-observation. You do this by first becoming aware of your competitive anxiety and admitting to it. All athletes feel anxiety. To combat this, you need to anticipate the anxiety by creating a plan to deal with it. There are many ways to manage anxiety, including deep breathing, reassuring self-talk ("I will be okay," "things will work out," "I must not be too hard on myself") or confidence building statements you repeat to yourself and talking out your fears with a trusted other. Coping skills can help, but you first must see that they are more effective than drugs and greatly reduce risks of harm that drugs pose. You will quickly learn that talking it out or using a variety of coping skills work more effectively than drugs and they do not have any side effects.

Recommended Reading

Leon Wurmser's 1978 book The Hidden Dimension, published by Jason Aronson.

References

Freud, A. (1966) *The Ego and The Mechanisms of Defense* (trans. C. Baines). International Universities Press.

Freud, S. (1911–1913). *The Standard Edition of the Complete Psychological Works of Sigmund Freud Vol. XII.* W.W. Norton & Company.

Kelly, G. (1992) *The Psychology of Personal Constructs.* Vol. 1 Theory and Personality. Routledge.

McGoldrick, M. (1996) *Irish Families. In Ethnicity and Family Therapy*, 2nd Ed. Eds. McGoldrick, M., Giordano. J., and Pearce, J. The Guilford Press.

Roberts, B. & Myers, J. Religion, National Origin, Immigration and Mental Illness. *American Journal of Psychiatry*, 110, 10(1954) 759–764.

Wadler, G. & Hainline, B. (1989) *Drugs and the Athlete.* F.A. Davis Company.

Wurmser, L. (1978) *The Hidden Dimension.* Jason Aronson.

6 Grandiosity, Self-idealization and Narcissism in the Athlete

Self-idealization or grandiosity is a defense common to athletes with narcissistic personalities. Self-idealization means attributing exaggerated greatness to oneself. Unfortunately, for those who use this kind of defense, what comes along with this is self-devaluation or the assigning of extreme negative qualities to the self. These two defensive positions are wedded and occur in the narcissist who is unable to tolerate average performance. They feel they are either great or atrocious with no toleration of any in between state. Narcissistic characters are drawn to sports where the playing field offers them an audience and a chance to acquire recognition, applause and affirmation of their greatness. And one can add, this takes place without the risk of interpersonal closeness.

It is relatively easy to spot this defense when working with the narcissist. One gets a sense that you are not being listened to. The narcissist will defend against all feelings of connection and dependency, and the therapist will frequently observe them yawning, a sign of interpersonal disconnection. In addition, the countertransference means that the therapist will feel bored and disengaged as well. The narcissist has a very primitive psychological structure and sports provides them with adequate stimulation and an escape from their inner emptiness and isolation.

> Yawning is commonly seen with narcissists and is a sign of a defense against affect, dependency and closeness. I have frequently seen this reaction with high-level golfers I have worked with. Ordinarily, when working with an athlete for extended periods, one expects growing trust, openness and an easy emotional exchange. But with the narcissistic athlete, the affect remains superficial as does the content of the exchange. Any question, whether it is as non-threatening and vague as "how are you doing?" to more penetrating and personal questions like "what's your reaction to your loss this week?" will be met with

> a yawn. Yawning shows that the athlete's defenses are in operation and being enlisted to keep them away from you. Since this reaction is so repetitive, one has plenty of chances to explore the issue by questions such as "Why do you think you yawn?", "Is yawning telling us something?" Or "What do you think yawning means?"

The athlete's self-idealization gives them confidence and is a powerful defensive shield, and in many ways, this defense is very helpful for competitive sports (Modell, 1986). However, as I stated, there is also a down side to this character trait since their grandiosity implies that they must perform perfectly or else they feel a sense of devaluation, rage and shame. The quest for the idealized perfect performance is common in sports, and when the therapist sees this in a patient, they are often in the presences of a narcissistic athlete who is internally saddled with the demand to be perfect. Should the athlete fail to be perfect, they often plummet into conscious and unconscious self-attack which is termed self-devaluation. The narcissistic athlete who uses self-idealization is not able to understand that they will play well some days but fail on other days. They suffer what is referred to as vertical splits where they either feel superhuman or subhuman (Kohut, 1975). He stated that, with narcissistic patients, mirroring of the patient's self-worth needs to be maintained for them to eventually internalize a sense of worth and give up the perfectionist idealistic demands and the devaluation they experience on a daily basis. In the following case, I will explain how I used the Kohutian approach to help the athlete to understand how his defenses have been formed.

Case Study: This is the case of a 16-year-old soccer player who presented with symptoms of depression, extreme self-doubt, self-criticism and perfectionism. He was a talented high school player who was a striker on the team and over the last few months had become more sullen, withdrawn and self-attacking. His negativity had become so bad that he would sometimes cry if he failed to score in a game. In school, he was a straight A student. He describes his mother as 'serious' and had a very supportive father, and he was the younger sibling to a gifted older brother. He was well respected by teammates but had become increasingly more withdrawn, sullen and anxious to the point of wanting to quit the game. With this mounting crisis, the father brought him in for a consult, desperate to find help and direction. As I got to know this young player, he described himself as extremely demanding, and if he did not do well in any endeavor, he would regress to childlike demeanor of shaking, quivering and then finally withdrawing. This dynamic was apparent within the first session after I had asked him to describe an experience he had in soccer. He felt he had described it to me poorly and first became angry with himself and then began to cry. His grandiose expectations were so extreme that they had contaminated virtually all areas of his life and now even a benign question had to be perfectly answered. Since answering anything perfectly was impossible, he immediately plummeted into devaluation and despair.

This case showed in a dramatic fashion how an athlete whose self-idealization defense had been so thoroughly extreme and untenable that now any perceived flaw led to immediate devaluation. Despite the obvious need for therapy, and as is often the case with grandiose athletes, this patient terminated prematurely after only ten sessions. It may be that he and his father realized that further exploration would inevitably lead to dependency which he did not want. Narcissists abhor dependency. If this case did proceed, it would have done so in the following steps. We would have tried to outline how self-idealization leads to devaluation. With insight, we also would have been working on the building of the working alliance which would have provided him with good enough mirroring to aid him in understanding that his performance need not be perfect to be good enough. This would have entailed then teaching him forgiveness. I hasten to add that this case is instructive in being so typical. Premature terminations are exceedingly common both in clinical psychology and even more so in sport psychology, and it is essential that the therapist does not take these premature terminations as a sign that they are doing something poorly or that their interventions are weak. What is weak in these cases is the narcissistic self-idealizing athlete's ability to trust.

Key Points

- Self-idealization is commonly known as grandiosity and can be a helpful defense for the athlete if used only on occasion.
- The defense of self-idealization implies a narcissistic character structure.
- Often, self-idealization is accompanied by self-devaluation if performance is not perfect.
- Yawning during sessions is a sign that the athlete is self-idealizing and is defending against closeness.
- It is wise to mirror their strength in order to build a working alliance, something they will resist.

Reflective Questions

- Describe the attitude of the narcissistic athlete and explain why they are difficult to treat.
- Why does self-idealization always come with self-devaluation?

- Describe why you think yawning is a sign you are facing a narcissist.
- Why do you think trust is so difficult to establish in an athlete who is grandiose?

Tips for Best Performance

If you are a perfectionistic and fall into despair and rage when you lose, it is a sign that you are far too demanding on yourself. You need to explore your self-attacks and modify them.

Exercise Drills for Best Performance

- If you are a perfectionistic and rage against yourself too often, this may be a sign that you are unconsciously overidealizing yourself and expect too much. A good drill is to get into the habit of displacing your self-attack onto something else. Curse the wind, the ball or even the Gods above. Displacement of anger outside of yourself will serve to protect your self-esteem.
- If you are in the habit of devaluing yourself after you make mistakes, do what Tiger Woods learned to do by permitting yourself to be angry for ten seconds only and then let it go and return to focus attention.

Recommended Reading

Andrew Morrison's 1986 essay "Shame, Ideal Self and Narcissism" in Essential Papers on Narcissism Ed. Andrew Morrison New York University Press.

References

Kohut, H. (1977) *The Restoration of the Self*. International Universities Press.
Modell, A. (1986) A Narcissistic Defence Against Affects and the Illusion of Self-Sufficiency. In *Essential Readings in Narcissism* (Ed. A. Morrison). New York University Press, 293–307.

7 Depersonalization in a Golfer

Depersonalization is a dissociation defense when one's thoughts and feelings seem to be unreal or not belonging to oneself. This prevents the athlete from staying focused (Gabbard, 2010). Depersonalization is defined as the defense of disruption of identity, consciousness or thinking, and this defense is highly problematic for an athlete who must remain in touch with their natural ability, identity and thought process during the flow of competition. Depersonalization has been described as becoming detached from the self and the world begins to seem vague. This is a primitive but not rare state with as many as 75% of adults experiencing it at one time in their life (Gabbard, 2010). It can last for a few minutes or up to hours or days.

Case Study: This is a case of a 17-year-old female golfer who was brought in by her father who recognized that something was wrong with his daughter's play. The athlete complained of "not being herself" on the course and of being unable to get into rhythm as she swung. She described this state as "overthinking" and like she was in a fog and numb. She felt "weird" when this occurred and she would grow quiet. If she had to play when she felt depersonalized, she would perform on a subpar level. This would last for a few hours at a time and occurred once or more per week. When we first started to work together, she was in this state chronically as she played and it was reflected with overthinking, hesitation, non-aggressive play. Despite this overwhelming state, her talent allowed her to keep playing. Initially, as we worked together, she would not admit to me the nature of her state of mind and would simply say she was "overthinking," but over the course of a year or more, she was able to admit with more accuracy the nature of her depersonalized state. At the outset, we were able to manage the dissociation by encouraging her to be more vocal, more jocular and more aggressive on the course which worked fairly well.

We endeavored to discover when this depersonalized state was first used. She recalled her experiences as a child which included her being chronically sexually abused by a grandfather who lived in the home with them. She taught herself to depersonalize and ignore the abuse by imagining she was a part of the cartoon show "My Little Pony." This took place throughout her early childhood and was a necessary and effective defense which permitted her to survive the abuse. However, she was forced to overuse this defense on a daily basis. She did not develop schizoid fantasies, multiple personality or severe memory loss, but her overuse of depersonalization was now, 10 years later, proving to be problematic as she played golf.

> Multiple Personality Disorder: The most severe form of depersonalization and dissociation is seen with multiple personality disorders, a relatively rare disorder usually established when a child experiences severe abuse. In multiple personality, the patient will split into a different identity, and when they return to normal, there will be no recall of who they were and of what occurred. It is similar to a black out state but without the use of alcohol. These different identities within a person will have different names and wear different clothes. I have treated patients with multiple personality disorder, a diagnosis that usually takes about seven years to make. Multiple personality was described in the Gothic horror novella "The Stange Case of Dr. Jekyll and Mr. Hyde" written by Robert Louis Stevenson. However, mild depersonalization is far more common and felt by many. It is described as feeling far away, different or in a fog. It has been my experience that patients who report this style of thinking are typically above average in IQ (Chase, 1987).

One can see how this kind of defense serves a positive effect by protecting a child from feeling too much terror, pain or anxiety, but when the child begins to overuse it, due to the chronicity of the chaotic environment, they get stuck in this defense style rather than getting past it by developing more mature defenses such as humor, anticipation, repression, suppression or self-assertion.

This player was locked into this depersonalized defense which was preventing her from anticipating and planning for game time. And as is often the case, her vagueness and withdrawn quality was misdiagnosed as attention deficit and she was placed on stimulants which had little impact on her fogginess, vagueness, lack of focus, anxiety or depersonalization.

Standard protocols used to help patients with depersonalization include anchoring methods such as chatting or listening to music to distract them. I used this along with standard therapy to help her gain insights as to the cause and onset of this defense and move beyond it. She began to use humor on the course to replace her depersonalized "overthinking" defense.

Key Points

- Depersonalization is a form of defense which alters one's sense of identity or thinking for a brief period.
- The athlete who uses this defense describes themselves as feeling "weird" or "not myself."
- The cause of this defense often stems from a chaotic, abusive or contentious home environment which induced the athlete to depersonalize or remove themselves psychologically.
- The use of depersonalization and dissociation is seen in high-IQ athletes.
- Insight as to the cause of this defense followed by anchoring techniques, humor and anticipation defenses are very helpful.

Reflective Questions

- How would you define the depersonalization defense and why is it used?
- Name two movies which had characters which used this defense. (Hint: one film had a psychiatrist who used depersonalization.)
- The technique of hypnosis temporarily enlists the depersonalization defense in subjects. Explain.
- Why is the defense of depersonalization associated with high intelligence?

Tips for Best Performance

If you find yourself spaced out, becoming silent, in a fog, odd or "not yourself," you may be experiencing depersonalization. This is a defense which was once used by you to help you to cope. Sharing our concerns about this state with a parent or sport psychologist will be helpful. Anchoring techniques such as listening to music or making statements to oneself that anchor you back to reality can be helpful.

Exercise Drill for Best Performance

- If you find yourself spaced out, becoming silent, in a fog, feeling odd, out of sync with conversations or "not yourself," you may be experiencing depersonalization. This is a defense which was once used by you to help you to cope. You can use a variety of distraction techniques to snap out of this defense which is always just a temporary state. You can joke around or listen to your favorite music. Sharing your concerns about this state with a friend, parent or psychoanalyst will be helpful.

- Ironically, being in the zone shares characteristics with the defense of depersonalization in that you enter your own private world when in the zone. To get in the zone, one needs to separate from your surroundings by ignoring others and focusing exclusively on your game. We are social animals, and so, it is surprisingly difficult to separate from others psychologically. If you are a golfer, you can practice this by not looking at your opponent when they swing, and better yet, not talking to them throughout the round. Anika Sorenstam was trained in this technique, and it helped her to enter the zone and win more.

Recommended Reading

Robert Louis Stevenson's "The Strange Case of Dr. Jekyll and Mr. Hyde".

References

Chase, T. (1987) *When Rabbit Howls*. E.P. Dutton.
Gabbard, G. (2010) *Long-Term Psychodynamic Psychotherapy: A Basic Text*. American Psychiatric Publishing.

8 Autistic Fantasies in a Long-Distance Swimmer

Autistic fantasy is defined as a defense of retreating into one's private internal world to avoid anxiety about personal relations (Gabbard, 2010). A famous example of the use of autistic fantasy is Ben Hogan who had an alter ego he referred to as "Hennie Bogan." Hogan's history of loneliness and loss, his work ethic and his self-imposed nickname offer some evidence that Hogan used autistic fantasy as a defense (Ferraro, 2010). The use of a vivid childhood imaginary playmates is considered to be an autistic fantasy defense. This defense allows an imaginary object to substitute fully for a real relationship that has been lost. Sigmund Freud (1926) first described this defense and George Valliant (1992) expanded upon it. It is not unusual to see this tendency in children who have experienced great loss and aloneness.

To understand why some athletes resort to this primitive defense, we can note how Ben Hogan witnessed the suicide of his father when he was six years old. This severe life-changing trauma plunged the family into poverty and anxiety, and this may be where Hogan established his autistic fantasy and allowed him to remain psychologically intact. He became famous for being an extreme loner and workaholic. Hogan kept himself company with an inner dialogue and fantasy life which helped him to escape human connection and not feel too lonely.

Case Study: This is a case of a nationally ranked swimmer who came to me after his freshman year in college complaining of anxiety. In his last meet, he had passed out in the water and nearly drowned and was understandably anxious about swimming. When I asked him how this happened, he said that he knows how to push himself beyond his limits. This kind of discipline and work ethic is not unusual in elite athletes but then he did say something that got my attention. He made the remark "You would not want to be near me as a swim meet nears." I asked him why not, and he divulged that he became a different person and actually referred to himself with a different name. When I asked him what his fantasy name was, he said "The Animal." As we explored this nickname, he began to divulge his history. He was from a divorced home and his father was extremely abusive to him, administering verbal and physical abuse on a regular basis. The fear, the pain and the sadness that he endured forced him to create a fantasy life and a fantasy world run by "The Animal." In this world, he became "The Animal" and could feel no pain.

His extreme pain tolerance was demonstrated in the following story. I asked him how he paced himself in a 400-meter race. He told me most push themselves to the limit in the first and last legs but pace themselves in the two middle legs. He pushed himself to the limit in every leg.

> I swim as hard as I possibly can in lap one. I follow this by swimming as hard as possible in laps two and three. And I finish it off by pushing myself beyond my limits in the last lap.

This kind of punishment produced the passing out experience I referred to above. Swimming is an extremely solitary and demanding sport which requires hours of painful practice where you are in the water and left to your own thoughts. It is easy to see why those who can fantasize would benefit. Certain sports attract introspective athletes who fantasize themselves. Sports like golf, long-distance running, swimming and cycling are like that. One of the most imaginative writers alive today is Haruki Murakami who is also a marathon runner who wrote the book "What I Talk About When I Talk About Running: A Memoir."

> Haruki Murakami is a Japanese writer and marathon runner. He wrote many wild, imaginative and compelling novels, including "The Wind-Up Bird Chronicle," and they all demonstrate the vivid schizoid imagination of this writer. He also blessed us with one of his few non-fiction books, one about his experience as a marathon runner ("What I Talk About When I Talk About Running"). His writing about running reveals many things about him as an athlete and as a person. He remarks that he can't imagine anyone liking him but can easily imagine them hating him. This suggests to me that he is a loner who has sheltered himself from the world of others through both his writing and running. He says he is filled with solitude and uses running to heal his loneliness. I do not know Haruki Murakami personally but would not at all be surprised to learn that he used fantasy to keep himself company and to avoid interactions with fellow humans. Autistic fantasy life helps one to cope with loneliness.

Autistic fantasy is something that can be helpful to the athlete who must spend long hours alone developing his craft. The reasons that people develop autistic fantasy may relate to a history of abuse, loss, an unusually sensitive temperament or some combination of these three things. This is why autistic fantasy cannot be taught. In the world of golf, the closest we have to Hogan right now is Tiger Woods who also led a traumatic life as a child. He was the only black child in a white neighborhood. He was tied to trees and had racial epithets painted on his chest while in kindergarten (2005). And out of that pain arose a warrior who had as much focus and will power as Ben Hogan had. Woods has extraordinary focus which is palpable when you are with him. He has the uncanny ability to make you feel isolated and invisible when in his presence. The only way a person would be able to do that is if they have an internal fantasy life that is vivid and strong. As a child, Woods was a stutterer, wore glasses and was described as a nerd by his good friend Notah Begay who nicknamed Woods "Urkel" based upon the fictional TV character Steve Urkel in the show "Family Matters." Urkel was the character with thick glasses and wore flood pants held up by suspenders.

In the case in question here, the swimmer developed an autistic fantasy life as a child and used it to good effect in his long-distance swimming. However, it was so effective that he ignored pain and eventually passed out while swimming. We discussed this process, but once again, this was a short-term process for him and took place before Skype was around so the case only lasted one summer. He returned to school in the south and I lost touch with him.

Key Points

- Autistic fantasy is the retreat into a fantasy world in order to avoid anxiety caused by personal relationships.
- Ben Hogan is an example of a famous athlete who may have used autistic fantasy throughout his adult life.
- Autistic fantasy may be helpful in sports that require the athlete to spend long periods of time alone. This may include long-distance swimming, running and biking as well as golf, hiking and mountain climbing.

Reflective Questions

- Define the term autistic fantasy and give an example of it.
- Loneliness and social isolation are coped with through the use of imagination and fantasy. How do you manage your loneliness?
- Which sports call upon the use of autistic fantasy?

> **Tips for Best Performance**
>
> Conscious or unconscious schizoid fantasies about winning as the athlete nears the end of the round, the game or the race produce anxiety since it serves to overwhelm them with grandiose images of trophies and hearing the applause. In order to suppress this tendency and STAY IN THE MOMENT, one must be trained to do so. A drill I use is to teach athletes on how to stay in the present is to glimpse at the clock once in the morning, go about your morning rituals of coffee, showering, food intake, etc., get in the car and proceed to training camp, etc. Suppress the tendency to glance at the clock for reassurance that you will not be late. This gets you in the habit of ignoring scoreboard or clock watching.

Exercise Drills for Best Performance

Many unconscious fantasies about winning occur when victory is in sight. This inhibits focus and often produces anxiety by overwhelming them with grandiose images of trophies and applause. In order to suppress this tendency and *STAY IN THE MOMENT*, one must be trained to do so. A drill I use is to teach athletes on how to stay in the present is to become aware of these pleasant fantasies as they emerge and then suppress them immediately. You can use the technique of thought-stopping which simply means that you say 'CANCEL IT!' when you become aware of the winning fantasy and then get back to focus in the here and now. Do this every time you play, and over time, you will learn to suppress your fantasies and by so doing stay in the present.

Recommended Reading

Haruki Murakami's book "What I Talk About When I Talk About Running: A Memoir."

Ferraro, T. (2010) Digging It Out of the Dirt: Ben Hogan, Deliberate Practice and the Secret. In *Annual Review of Golf Coaching*, 65–68.

Freud, S. (1926) Inhibitions, Symptoms and Anxiety. In *Standard Edition of Complete Psychological Works of Sigmund Freud* (trans. and ed. J. Stachey). Hogarth Press, 20, 77–175.

Gabbard, G. (2010) *Long-term Psychodynamic Psychotherapy: A Basic Text. Second Edition*. American Psychiatric Publishing.

Tiger: The Authorized DVD, 2005.

Vailliant, G. (1992) *Ego Mechanisms of Defense: A Guide for Practitioners and Researchers*. American Psychiatric Press.

9 Perfectionism or the Splitting Defense in Athletes

The perfectionistic athlete is usually employing the splitting defense which means there is a failure to integrate positive and negative aspects of the self into a cohesive self-identity (DSM-5-TR, 2022). James Grotstein suggests that splitting is a universal phenomenon occurring throughout the lives of all individuals (Grotstein, 1985). Perfectionism is one aspect of splitting and is a common trait in professional sports. If an athlete appears to crumble and lose confidence after one or two mistakes, it is probably due to their use of the splitting defense. These athletes seem unable to recall the positive aspects of who they are as athletes and perceive any failure in performance as proof that they are an impostor, defective and weak. They are not able to integrate positive and negative aspects of themselves into a whole view.

Melanie Klein worked extensively on this defense and suggested that the infant's split awareness of their life and death instinct was the genesis of the splitting defense used in adult life (Klein, 1921). The defense of splitting is commonly referred to as black and white thinking. If the athlete is using this defense, they experience doubt, tension, anxiety and despair the moment they make a mistake. They have no self-object constancy. Athletes use perfectionistic grandiose fantasies to repress the enfeebled underlying negative sense of self. This is explained by Firestone and Catlett when they suggest that this defense is created during childhood in order to gain parental approval if the parents' love was conditional and only given if the child performed well (Firestone & Catlett, 1981). In highly accomplished young athletes with overinvolved parents, the defense of splitting is common since the mandate is to excel or get rejected.

Case Study: This professional golfer came to my office in great frustration. He was expected to be a standout on the PGA Tour but instead was now languishing on the Korn Ferry 'Tour', the minor league of golf. He demonstrated the following pattern of self-defeat. If he played well for the first few holes, he would have a good round since he relaxed, established confidence and dominated. But if he struggled within the first few holes, his

> The Mercedes commercial plays on the listener's use of the splitting defense with their slogan which repeats the phrase "Mercedes, the best or nothing at all." The successful use of a slogan like this enlists the consumers' primitive perfectionism and anxiety by suggesting that they are bereft of value if they do not drive a Mercedes. Advertisers employ highly trained psychologists to help write these ads. Edward Bernays was considered the father of public relations and not coincidentally was the nephew of Sigmund Freud. Bernays lived in the United States but spent every summer with Freud in Austria where he learned Freud's theories of defenses which repress our basic and childlike desires. Bernays was the first to employ Freud's theory of unconscious in public relations and advertising.

confidence evaporated quickly, his confidence was lost and he felt increasing anxiety, became tense and played poorly for the entire round. Sports are designed to be difficult and all athletes make mistakes; however, if an athlete tends to employ splitting and perfectionism, they will become tense and subject to despair and self-doubt during play. Despite being given a gamut of coping skills through seminars, these tips apparently did little good and he continued to be plagued by overreactions when he made a mistake like three putting on the first hole. I first offered him the standard sport psychology self-talk and relaxation tools but nothing seemed to have an impact. Over time, we began to discern how he used splitting which caused his performance to diverge in two diametrically different ways. If he was doing well, he felt confident and acted with cockiness and self-assurance. But if he made a bogey on the first or second hole, he quickly became a different player, doubted himself, began to overthink and hesitate. He would begin to steer his drives rather than swing freely. All of this is a disaster for a PGA Tour golfer since the courses they play are designed to punish weak shot making.

We came to understand that he was using the defense of splitting where he was either the grandiose self-inflated golfer or plummet into the self-devalued fraudulent weak player. There was no gray in his attitude toward himself. It was either all white or black, "the best or nothing at all," the language of the perfectionist. And as we talked about this, he began to articulate a more mature process of thinking with the realization that no one could hit every shot well and one does not need to be perfect to play good golf.

As we slowly gained insight into this, one should not believe that any one epiphany of insight into his defense of splitting would open the door toward rational thinking. It took us two years to work through this insight and that was with twice weekly sessions. Sigmund Freud understood the value of what he called "working through" insights.

> Freud pointed out the necessity of working through insights and pointed out that patterns of defense emerge again and again and must be repetitively interpreted, observed, confronted and clarified until at last the patient will accept the interpretations. Shafer (1983) also emphasized this point about working through by suggesting that one must have patience to face the endless series of repetitions, permutations, variations and regressions that patients present. This is especially problematic in sports where there is constant pressure to get the athlete ready for game day which may be only 24 hours away. The answer to that problem is to recognize that professional- and Olympic-level athletes have rare and unique talent and they have already invested perhaps ten years in preparation for their pro careers so that an investment which will allow them to be free of their inhibiting demons is well worth the effort in time and money.

One reasonable question is whether this athlete used a different defense after his splitting defense was worked through. In this case, the athlete developed a keener sense of self-observation (see Chapter 26). He reported to me that he felt stronger as a person over time which is a remark that many patients make after some time in therapy. It is always very difficult to articulate the process of cure and which aspects of treatment were crucial. When asked, they will say they feel stronger, freer, more independent or more solid both on and off the field. To use a term that Jean Piaget used to describe children's cognitive growth, over time, the athlete in depth sport psychology treatment seems to accommodate to a new way of feeling and a new way of being. We might call this ego strength. In this case, and in many cases of perfectionism, the working alliance is key because it emphasizes the enjoyment felt in working together which means that the athlete is finally receiving unconditional love rather than the conditional loved based upon performance that created the problem of splitting in the first place.

Key Points
- Perfectionism or the splitting defense is common in professional sports.
- This defense stems from a childhood where love was made contingent upon performance. Often times, the parents get so mesmerized with the child's talent and lose sight of the child's basic needs.

- Perfectionism and splitting implies black and white, or all or nothing thinking.
- Enjoying the work of therapy with the athlete gives them a feeling of being loved and respected and this is part of the cure.

Tips for Best Performance

If you notice yourself overreacting and focusing on minor mistakes, getting down on yourself too fast or failing to appreciate your accomplishments, you may be using the splitting defense which employs perfectionism. Try looking carefully at your overall performance to allow you to be more reasonable and more forgiving.

Reflective Questions

- How would you define perfectionism?
- Give two examples of perfectionism in sports from your personal experience.
- How does one overcome perfectionism?

Exercise Drills for Best Performance

- Exercise Drill #1: If you find yourself overreacting to minor mistakes, you need to learn to be realistic and therefore forgiving. Once per night spend ten minutes reviewing your positive accomplishments in sports. This can come from the day's performance or things that have occurred in your recent or distant past. The reason this is so important is that it is a systematic effort to develop self-esteem which is what you need to get beyond perfectionism and self-attack.
- Exercise Drill #2: A sign of mental health is the ability to self-observe in a realistic fashion (see Chapter 26, Self-observation in Athletes). This means to view any disruptive incident more broadly. To replace perfectionism with more realistic self-observation, get into the habit of saying to yourself "a small smudge on an otherwise beautiful canvas does not mean the picture becomes ugly. In fact, it makes the picture more interesting."

Recommended Reading

James Grotstein's Splitting and Projective Identification.

References

DSM-5-TR (2022) *Diagnostic and Statistical Manual of Mental Disorders*. American Psychiatric Association.

Firestone, R. & Catlett, J. (1981) *Psychological Defenses in Everyday life*. Human Sciences Press.

Grotstein, J. (1985) *Splitting and Projective Identification*. Jason Aronson.

Klein, M. (1921) *The Development of a Child. In Contributions to Psycho-Analysis, 1921–1945*. Hogarth Press.

Shafer, R. (1983) *The Analytic Attitude*. Basic Books.

10 Superstitious Behavior Used by the Regressed Athlete

Athletes use superstitious behaviors when feeling anxiety and uncertainty, and this type of behavior is an expression of regression. The defense mechanism of regression is defined as a response to anxiety by reverting back to earlier more childlike behavior. Regression is commonly seen when children who are fatigued revert to sucking their thumb or clinging to a teddy bear. Regression occurs in athletes with increases in drug taking, excessive advice seeking and the use of superstitious behavior such as wearing a certain color or eating a certain kind of food before games. Athletes will revert to superstitious behavior by believing an object or a private ritual will magically protect them, keep them calm and give them the strength to win. Margaret Mahler's discussion of transitional objects used by children helps us to understand regressive trends and why athletes regress to this kind of magical thinking.

> Margaret Mahler on the superstitious behavior of children: Margaret Mahler's groundbreaking work on separation/individuation outlined the normal developmental process all toddlers go through as they become ambulatory and begin to separate from the mother's side (Mahler, 1968). Their ability to walk allows them to gain distance from the mother, but this also induces anxiety which is usually dealt with by selecting a teddy bear or security blanket for comfort and a feeling of safety as a substitute for the mother. She referred to these things as transitional objects since they served to ease the pain of transition during separation and development. Eventually, the teddy bear is given up as the toddler develops maturity and is able to internalize confidence.

Regressive use of objects such as good luck charms, magical rituals or other forms of childlike dependency are unconscious efforts to feel safe, find courage and be strong. These superstitions function similar to the placebo effect in medicine where, if a patient is told they will feel relief from pain by a prescribed pill, they often do feel relief. However, the difference between a magic charm and a placebo pill is that there is an experienced, credentialed trusted doctor who is administering the pill but with superstitious behavior, it is the athlete themselves who are prescribing the magic. The athlete's defensive superstitious efforts tend to be ineffective because their overuse prevents more adaptive ways of coping with competitive stress. It is important to come to an understanding of why the athlete has resorted to superstitious rituals and magic to cope with stress.

To replace the superstitious rituals, sport psychologists typically provide a series of coping skills which will include positive self-talk, relaxation therapy or rational emotive therapy. If the psychologist is trusted and respected by the athlete, the coping skills can have a placebo-like impact. However, if the athlete is in a regressed state and no insight has been gained as to what caused this regression, then coping skills will lose their magic quickly. When regressive defenses are explored and the reasons for their use are understood, this will allow the athlete to take in and learn from the coping mechanisms taught to them. Usually, athletes who are prone to regressive superstitious behavior have had overinvolved parents who failed to foster independence but instead enabled and reinforced regression and dependency.

Case study: This case involves an LPGA star who adamantly held to the superstition that she must eat only chicken the night before a tournament, have two cups of coffee before the round and carry only 7 tees in her pocket. Her history revealed that she was overly dependent on her father who was critical of her, rarely gave approval and was overinvolved with her career. All of these quaint rituals seem harmless enough until put in their meaningful context. All of her rituals were employed as just so many magical security blankets and revealed that she was not individuated but rather was stuck in that in-between phase and had not fully separated. She was in need of individuation and all of the superstitions and magic chicken is not going to help that. This LPGA star was using her magical superstitions in order to forgo the chance to actually work on what was causing her anxiety through discussion with me. She used her magic to remain fixated at a younger age and thereby avoid the chance to mature and to discuss what was plaguing her in reality. So far, we have not been able to discuss her regressive use of her lucky talisman and her lucky dietary rituals and she continues to use the ritual without any apparent benefit. I eventually came to realize that she used this kind of regressed magical transitional object in order to avoid dependency on me or anyone else who might abuse her or create dependency like her father did.

In these cases, we see evidence of a disturbed relationship with a parent who was overinvolved or abusive and how this made the athlete vulnerable to regression and the use of magical thinking and using superstitious behavior as a way of coping with anxiety. Regression or reverting to childlike ways of behaving is common among athletes, and the method of treatment is to help them to understand the circumstances which led to their regressive vulnerability. Understanding the true nature of their behavior and what led up to it goes a long way in helping them to grow and develop a more mature manner of coping with stress. It can be argued that superstitious rituals like knocking on wood, carrying a lucky rabbit's foot or making the sign of the cross before stepping into the batter's box are harmless and can be comforting to the athlete. However, when these superstitious rituals are used to resist connection with a real therapist, then all efforts to teach standard mental skills or developing more mature defenses will remain impossible.

Key Points

- Superstitious behavior is a sign that the athlete feels uncertain and anxious.
- Superstitious rituals come in many forms, including carrying magical or 'lucky' objects, wearing certain colors, saying prayers or eating only certain foods.
- Superstitious behavior is a sign that the athlete is in a regressed state.

Reflective Questions

- How would you define superstitious behavior and what is its purpose?
- Can you list three common superstitious behaviors?
- Do you think superstitious behavior works, and if so, why?
- Do you think superstitious behavior is ineffective, and if so, why?
- Why do you think the use of superstitious behavior like eating certain foods or wearing certain types of clothing is so common?

Tips for Best Performance

Although superstitious behavior may be mildly or temporarily effective, it is best to spend time preparing for the event and understanding that a trained athlete is a tough athlete. It is also wise to learn more adaptive coping skills such as deep breathing, distraction techniques, the use of humor and suppressive techniques.

Exercise Drill for Best Performance

- If you are using superstitious behaviors like special diets, rituals or charms, it is likely that you are trying to deal with anxiety and that you feel helpless and worried about making mistakes. Although superstitious behavior may be mildly effective, it is best to spend time more preparing for the event and making sure you realize that you have done your prep work and reassure yourself that you are ready. It is also wise to use more adaptive coping skills such as deep breathing, distraction techniques, positive self-talk and the use of humor. Prior to every event, rehearse one or more of these more adaptive coping skills and use them when needed.

Recommended Reading

D.W. Winnicott's Playing and Reality published in 1971 by Routledge.

Reference

Mahler, M. (1968) *On Human Symbiosis and the Vicissitudes of Individuation*. International Universities Press.

11 Regression in a Professional Soccer Team

Regression as defined in the previous chapter is a reversion to a more childlike form of behavior. Wilfred Bion is the pioneer on group dynamics and felt that regression was an inevitable part of being in a group or team (Bion, 1968). When players become members of a team, they will regress to a more childlike state since a team environment mimics the family environment with coach as a parental figure and team members as siblings. When team members have tantrums, expect special attention, show jealousy and display inappropriate rivalries with other team members, these behaviors are a sign of regression. Wilfred Bion suggested that regression in groups occurs because membership inevitably triggers childhood feelings of being a part of a family. Bion felt there were three primary ways of regressing on team and he called these basic assumptions, including dependency, fight/flight and pairing. All of these forms of regression work against the basic task of the team which is to cooperate and win games. Wilfred Bion's writings on regressive behavior in groups will be used to explain the player behaviors that are elaborated in this chapter about a professional soccer team I worked with. Bion's basic assumption of dependency and fight/flight revealed how this team was crippled by having a teammate, who was one of the best soccer strikers in the world. However, his talent elicited passivity and jealousy in the rest of the team. His presence engendered both a sense of dependency and a sense that he would alone be able to fight for them and win games. These two repressive tendencies are two of the primary basic assumptions that Bion used to describe why groups frequently lose focus, become inefficient and off-task.

    I could see fairly quickly that the group was doing three things simultaneously. They were in a dependency state, expected the team super star to do most of the work and provide them with comfort and an easy ride. In addition, they were in a fight/flight mode having decided unconsciously that the enemy was the uncomforting coach and that the new team leader would fight off the evil enemy from within. The coach reacted to this unconscious dilemma by drinking, which is a common acting out method

> The presence of Tiger Woods on every United States Ryder Cup team over the last 20 years has produced surprisingly negative results. The American teams are pitted against the best from Ireland and the UK, and at each biannual event, the Americans are heavily favored since on paper they are invariably the more talented, earn more money and have won more events. However, the US team continues to underperform in these events to the consternation and confusion of the team leaders in charge. They valiantly try to change strategies each time, using "pods" which mimic the way they do at SEALS military training. However, no matter what the change in strategy, the team loses and any American player paired with Tiger Woods seems to underperform dramatically. This dynamic is best explained with Wilfred Bion's Dependency Assumption which predicts that players in this team like setting would regress and tend to expect Woods to take over and save the day.
>
> Case Study: I was the sport psychologist for this professional basketball team. There was strife within the team according to both the GM and the Medical Director and they were underperforming. In my first meeting with the head coach, we discussed the reasons for the team's discontent and he remarked that he had hoped that the presence of one of basketball's greatest players should have placed them in first place standing in the league. I know that the team had much international talent, and when I met with the team as a whole, it was clear that the team was unhappy and indicated that they resented to coach and appeared to be scapegoating him. Some even went so far as to say they were intentionally trying to lose games in order to get him fired. Yet, he was essentially a competent coach with strong credentials.

used by many depleted and overwhelmed coaches. The team continued to act out their dependency, passivity and their anger which eventually did get the coach fired. The star player began to see me twice weekly for support in his efforts to deal with these issues and he continues to see me today, some 20 years later.

In cases like this, professional team sport psychologists are given little opportunity to intervene in team meetings since the player's time availability is extremely limited and sport psychology continues to be undervalued and resisted. One is often left with curbside interventions prior to the players boarding a bus or a plane. One can merely observe how the acting out and the regressive behaviors unfold and try to deal with the multitude of variables that result. Needless to say, the treatment interventions to remediate these dynamics are complex, and given the minimal time given to sport psychology interventions, the actual treatment of teams awaits us in the distant future.

As the eminent psychoanalyst Kenneth Eisold once remarked "to belong is to regress." He believed that the irreducible and unavoidable dilemma experienced in groups is a return to more childlike regressive attitudes (Eisold, 1985). He suggested that although Wilfred Bion's work is discredited in America, we can ill afford to ignore his profound and revolutionary theories. For now, all we can do is to simply do our best to gain understanding of how these basic assumptions take place in teams. The future awaits us where there will be a time with greater understanding of how and why players regress on teams and what to do about it. Until then, we can expect to witness these inexplicable forms of childish tantrums, jealousy and self-defeat on teams who are constantly underperforming and failing to live up to their highly paid potential. This subject would make for a good series of Ph.D. dissertations in either clinical psychology or sport psychology. I work in the New York metropolitan area of the United States where there are 14 professional sports franchises, including two National Football League teams, two National Basketball Association teams, two National Hockey League teams, two Major League Baseball teams, one Women's National Basketball team and one Major Soccer League team. These teams all have huge yearly budgets fueled by wealthy owners, lucrative television contracts and major corporate sponsorship. Yet, despite budgets that match or exceed most of the other teams in their leagues, they all come up short of championships year after year. The only exception was a brief run by the New York Yankees in the last 1990s, thanks to the interesting combination of G.M. George Steinbrenner and head coach Joe Torres. There is only one way to account for all of this loss.

It is clear to me that GMs and head coaches do not have clue as to what to do about toxic self-defeating team dynamics reported weekly by the press. Many years ago, I was on a panel in New York City discussing team sports. A fellow panelist had run into a GM from one of the major New York teams in the area and invited him to attend the conference. What the GM said and I quote, "Why would I want to go there and listen to those wackos talk nonsense?" This is the typical resistance professional teams have concerning psychoanalysis. It matters not at all that they throw away hundreds of millions of dollars each year hiring the best coaches and players money can buy. As Freud wisely remarked many years ago, people see psychoanalysis as a plague that must be avoided at all costs. Players, coaches and GMs would rather lose games and money than look within themselves and discover what lurks there.

Regression on teams remains a constant problem for every team in professional and collegiate sports. This is poorly understood, complex and

58 Immature Defenses

under-researched area. As I said above, the study of team dynamics and team regression would make for an important series of dissertation projects.

Key Points

- Team members often regress because there is pull toward childhood behaviors since the team triggers memories and attitudes from their family of origin.
- Wilfred Bion's pioneering work on group dynamics helps explain why so many teams underperform, get lazy, are filled with jealousy and get off-task.
- Basic assumption of dependency is when the team unconsciously creates a leader whom they then depend upon for nurturance. If the leader does not provide this nurturance, there is a backlash of anger.
- Basic assumption of fight/flight is when a team sees its leader as either evil or all knowing.
- Basic assumption of pairing is when a team establishes a pair of leaders which embody the hope that this pair will produce a new solution to a problem. In all three basic assumptions, the group regresses into passivity and non-productivity.

Reflective Questions

- How would you define regression?
- Why do you think players regress when they join teams?
- Give an example of what Bion's basic assumption of dependency would look like on a team.
- Why is there so much infighting and backstabbing on teams?

Tips for Best Performance

If you are on a team that is filled with jealousy, laziness or infighting, do your best to ignore it all and become a team leader who focuses on the task at hand, which is to cooperate, support each other and work hard.

Exercise Drills for Best Performance

- Chances are if you're on a team you see either jealousy, laziness or infighting. If you see players acting jealously, you can set a good example by becoming a team leader and do not gossip or join in the jealousy.

- If you see you a team acting in a lazy, passive, non-focused way, once again become a team leader and set a good example to separating from the childish laziness and staying upbeat, working hard and remaining focused.

Recommended Reading

Wilfred Bion's chapter from Experiences in Groups In Group Relations Reader 1. Edited by Arthur Colman and W. Harold Bexton. A.K. Rice Institute.

References

Bion, W. (1968) *Experiences in Groups*. Routledge.
Eisold, K. (1985) Recovering Bion's Contributions to Group Analysis. In *Group Relations Reader 2* (Eds. A. Colman & M. Geller). A.K. Rice Institute, 37–48.

12 Somatization in Athletes

> The sorrow that has no vent in tears makes other organs weep.
>
> Henry Maudsley, anatomist 19th Century

Somatization is defined as the defensive conversion of emotional states into bodily symptoms. This defense is commonly referred to as a psychosomatic reaction and is categorized as immature defense. Somatization is expressed in a variety of ways, including difficulty swallowing, abdominal pain, nausea, bloating, diarrhea, difficulty urinating, food sensitivity, pain in back or joints, headaches, weakness or paralysis in the limbs, shortness of breath, chest pain, dizziness, hemorrhoids and arthritic flair ups. Somatization has also been referred to as masked depression expressed with headaches, back pain or gastrointestinal pain (Watts, 1968).

With this defense, the body is then assigned the task of coping with overwhelming emotions which enables the athlete's ego state and identity to remain stable in the face of extreme stress. One reason that team trainers are so popular with athletes is that they provide massages which relieve the psychosomatic tightness that so many athletes feel. I do not think there is much awareness on the part of the trainers or the athletes that the massages are enlisted to rub out the psychologically induced psychosomatic pain.

Felix Deutsch was an early pioneer in the field of psychosomatic disorders and the mysterious link between mind and body (Deutsch, 1959). More recently, Paul Shorter, history professor at the University of Toronto provided epidemiological data showing how common psychosomatic disorders are in the general population (Shorter, 1994). In my research (Ferraro, 1993), I interviewed 400 patients about the precursors to their psychosomatic reactions and discovered that about 90% had some short-term psychosomatic reaction in any 30-day period (Ferraro, 1999).

The French psychoanalyst Joyce McDougall has described the genesis of this defense deriving from experiences of overwhelming affect in early childhood which threatened the child's integrity and identity (McDougall, 1989). The overall physical sensitivity in the gifted athlete may set them up for this kind of early childhood shattering which then produces the establishment of the somatization defense.

In Phyllis Greenacre's essay "The Childhood of the Artist" (1971), she suggested that the gifted, and this includes the athletically gifted, have a different developmental trajectory than the average person. Extreme sensitivity of their perceptual and sensory apparatus produces in them extreme attachments to visual, kinesthetic or auditory experiences which precludes emotional attachments and may account for the alexithymic, unemotional and psychosomatic persona of so many gifted athletes (see text box below).

I will present a few cases which will demonstrate how the somatization defenses are enlisted to manage emotions in athletes.

Case #1: This case involves an alexithymic South Korean golfing star who suffered with migraine headaches, gastrointestinal pain and hives throughout her career. Childhood reveals she had an abusive father and her mother was neglectful and inadequate. Her demeanor was consistently pleasant, smiling and upbeat with an ability to banter and joke with me. Despite this pleasant easygoing nature in the transference, and despite her remarkable ability on the golf course, she chose to remain isolated from her peers, and as a result, she was labeled a loner and tended to be marginalized and scapegoated. Prior to many tournaments, she would vomit, have gastrointestinal pain and sometimes have migraine headaches. This was evidence of her use of the somatization defense to cope with emotional stress and her avoidance of teammates also supported the conclusion that social interaction in general produced overwhelming affect that she was not able to manage so she avoided interactions at all times. The manifestation of gastrointestinal pain, vomiting and migraines in addition to occasional hives which appeared on her abdomen were all part of her use of somatization to manage the variety of stresses she had to face, including playing in major championships. When an athlete is not able to manage emotions cognitively, they may resort to somatization to express, ventilate and simultaneously repress these emotions. The player would occasionally complain of uterine pain and had many sonograms and Magnetic Resonance Imaging's (MRIs) all of which were negative. This issue is again a somatic expression of the emotional pain of having no children. To rectify these issues took time and we did this by discussing the somatic symptoms when they emerged, tracing them back to their meanings and roots and helping the athlete to create better coping skills vis a vis emotions.

> Alexithymia is the condition where there is a paucity of affect-naming in the speech of some athletes (Sifneos, 1991). Alexithymic patients tend to be impersonal, cool, quirky and robotic. In their way of free associating, they show a remarkable lack of awareness of their emotions. A good example of an alexithymic response to obvious emotional upheaval was seen in an interaction I had with a PGA player who was leading the U.S. Open after three rounds. He performed very poorly on the last day or as athletes describe it "he threw up all over himself." When we spoke after the event, I asked him how he felt trying to hold onto the lead on the final day and he quickly and defensively remarked. "Oh, I wasn't nervous." In fact, he had no conscious experience of anxiety but clearly his body did. Another good example of alexithymia in an athlete occurred when I spoke to a golfer prior to him playing in the U.S. Open. I asked him what his biggest concern was as the week approached, and he said "My biggest worry is what am I going to have for dinner each night."

<u>Case #2</u>: This is a case of a third string NFL kicker who somatized his anxiety with nausea and vomiting before entering the game. The common experience of vomiting in sports was highlighted in the film "Any Given Sunday" starring Al Pacino as a head coach of an NFL football team and Jamie Foxx as his rookie quarterback. Jamie Foxx plays the character Willie "Steamin" Beaman who vomits on the sidelines before he enters the game. In the case of my patient, his vomiting was a concern of his coach which is why my services were sought. The patient's history indicated that both of his parents were intrusive into all aspects of his life. They were overly controlling and did not appear to be able to mirror him or attune to his emotional needs. Over time, it became evident to me that both parents were high functioning narcissists who used him for their own needs. This became exacerbated as he became more well-known and they attempted to participate in his glory. Joyce McDougall who suggested that when an infant has too many emotional disappointments due to maternal lack of attunement, the infant will defend against any emotional experience by using their body to handle stress. This establishes the somatization defense with the body permanently enlisted to handle feelings, thereby preventing other ways of coping. If an athlete does not know how to label, think about or talk about emotions, it is impossible for them to learn any new coping skill, no matter how carefully it is taught to them. It took a very long time to help this athlete overcome his psychosomatic reactions, and it was only after two years of twice weekly work that we made a dent into this problem.

He would often remark to me that the only time he had freedom to think or speak his mind was during the two 45-mintue sessions he had each week.

As he gained control over it, he was assigned to be lead kicker one game in mid-season. As he readied himself for game day, the night before he took an ice bath, and as he was raising himself out of the ice tub, he slashed his right toe. This successfully postponed his debut for the remainder of the season. As Freud would often say "There are really no such thing as 'accidents'." They are often dictated by unconscious fears or conflicts. In this case, the kicker was understandably terrified of starting and though he had overcome his somatization tendencies, that did not mean he was ready and willing to put himself under extreme pressure. He still was not able to discuss his emotions so he resorted to action, in this case an accident. This is another example of why standard cognitive behavioral sport psychology misses the mark. Try as you might to help the athlete talk about worries and concerns, if they are using the somatization defense and are alexithymic, the athlete really does not have useful access to positive self-talk or any other cognitive interventions since they are not aware of how they feel.

<u>Case #3</u> This amateur tennis player was in his mid-thirties when he came to my office due to underperforming and experiencing the serving yips when under pressure. He was a successful engineer who had a large practice on Long Island. He was extremely conscientious in his practice to the point of being compulsive. His compulsiveness came out in his tennis swing which was overcontrolled. He held the racket far too tightly, and though he was extremely fit and had a fine-looking serve, he lost racket speed because of his death grip.

Medically, his history indicated that he had suffered with diverticulitis ten years prior to seeing me which led to a re-sectioning of his small intestines due to the inflammation. He would often complain of back pain and neck pain which led him to many chiropractors in an effort to gain some relief from muscle spasms. His central complaint outside of tennis and his physical woes was that he was ignored at home both by his wife and three sons who treated him like a second-class citizen and gave him little respect. He gave them a lavish lifestyle, thanks to his hard work and expertise, but they failed to appreciate this. He had no voice in all matters at home. In the past, he had behavioral training to help him to repress some of his explosive outbursts and he conscientiously followed the behaviorist's direction and learned to suppress his anger totally. Shortly thereafter, he developed diverticulitis and colon re-sectioning. It appears that the total repression of emotional expression led to a regression into somatization, where the body took over the job of expressing emotions which produced the inflammation.

64 Immature Defenses

Why was he so prone to these psychosomatic problems, including diverticulitis, neck and back pain? Why was he unable to loosen his grip on the racket? It was all connected to his inability to feel and express his emotions. His maternal experience was similar to the last case discussed. The mother's lack of attunement had created in him the somatization defense whereby the body permanently took over the task of emotional expression. Whether he was anxious or angry, sad or happy, his body was enlisted as the way to express these emotions. This left him tongued at home and unable to learn other ways of dealing with stress on the court other than squeeze tight and hold on for dear life. This patient would always ridicule any suggestion I made about his physical state being the result of his emotions. We continue to work on a weekly basis.

> Hwabyeong is a Korean somatization disorder which arises when people are unable to confront their anger. This culture-bound syndrome includes symptoms of palpitations, dry mouth, insomnia, chest pressure, headaches and whole-body sensation of heat. The patient may be easily startled, sad, feeling guilt. It is frequently triggered by spousal infidelity or conflict with in-laws. The mechanism of the somatization defense is repression of anger.

In summary, somatization defense is common in athletes. In some ways, this lack of awareness of emotions can be a very helpful trait for the competitive athlete because it allows them to stay calm under pressure. I work with one PGA golfer who will win tournaments on occasion. If I am watching the event on TV as he stands over a five-foot putt to win, I will be experiencing anxiety, fear and tension. He always seems to make these tournament-winning putts, and afterward, I will ask him if he was anxious over the last putt to win, and he would say "Not really. It was an easy putt, no problem." The ability to screen out or ignore anxiety is a valuable defense for athletes, but often time, the underlying emotions will emerge and be felt somatically or with accident proneness. It is always wise to gain insight into where all that pain and muscle tension comes from.

Key Points

- Somatization defenses are often evidenced when athletes repeatedly complain of gastrointestinal symptoms like nausea, diarrhea, vomiting, abdominal pain, back or neck pain, migraines, weak limbs, chest pain, dizziness or are prone to accidents.

- Somatization means that the athlete cannot process feelings with his mind and so the body is enlisted to manage emotional states, including anxiety, despair, anger, joy or excitement.
- Somatic pain is sometimes referred to as masked or endogenous depression and is expressed with headaches, back pain or abdominal pain.
- Felix Deutsch was a pioneer who discussed the way bodily illness can be an expression of guilt, anxiety or repressed sadness.
- Joyce McDougall suggested that the causes of somatization derives from maternal failure which caused the child to close off emotional connections of all kinds.
- Even accident proneness can be considered a form of somatic defense.
- A weakness of somatization as defense is that the emotions that have been repressed will emerge in other ways such as displacement.

Reflective Questions

- How would you define somatization?
- Can you think of any somatic reactions that you are experiencing this week?
- Why do you think athletes are so prone to somatization?
- Can you think of a better way to cope with emotions instead of placing them in your body?

Tips for Best Performance

If you are a coach in charge of a team, chances are you have more than one athlete who is suffering from alexithymia and somatization. This athlete needs patient handling and must be put in the hands of a empathic assistant coach, trainer doctor or team psychologist who can devote time with him in order to repeatedly ask them to put into words how they are feeling at the time. Discovering what they are feeling is the key to helping the psychosomatic athlete. They need to learn how to discuss feelings rather than leaving it to their bodies to do the emotional work and the emotional suffering.

Exercise Drills for Best Performance

Exercise Drill #1: If you are a coach, chances are you have more than one athlete who is suffering with somatization. This athlete needs to ventilate their emotions rather than holding them in. Connect these athletes with an empathic assistant coach, trainer, doctor or team psychologist who can devote time to the athlete, listen to their emotional expression and encourage the athlete to verbalize their emotions. If the athlete does not learn to verbalize their emotions, they will enlist their bodies to do the emotional work which means an organ system will become hyper or hyperactivated will suffer.

Recommended Reading

"On the Mysterious Leap from the Mind to the Body" (1959) Edited by Felix Deutsch, M.D. International University Press.
   "Theaters of the Body; A Psychoanalytic Approach to Psychosomatic Illness" (1989) Joyce McDougall W.W. Norton and Company.

References

Deutsch, F. (1959) The Riddle of the Mind-Body Correlations. In *On the Mysterious Leap from the Mind to the Body, A Study on the theory of Conversion* (Ed. F. Deutsch). International Universities Press.

Ferraro, T. (1993) The Collapse of Culture, Psychosomatics and Narcissism. *The Psychoanalytic Psychotherapy Review*, 4(1): 1–31.

Ferraro, T. (1999) *Somatization During Separation and Individuation*. Long Island Institute of Psychoanalysis Annual Scientific Award.

Greenacre, P. (1971) The Childhood of the Artist. In *Emotional Growth*, Vol. 2. International Universities Press, pp. 479–504.

McDougall, J. (1989) *Theaters of the Body, A Psychoanalytic Approach to Psychosomatic Illness*. W.W. Norton & Company.

Shorter, P. (1994) *From the Mind into the Body, the Cultural Origins of Psychosomatic Symptoms*. Maxwell Macmillan International.

Sifneos, P. (1991) Affect, Emotional Conflict and Deficit: An Overview. *Psychotherapy and Psychosomatics*, 56(3): 116–122.

Watts, C. (April, 1968) The Evoltion of Depressive Symptoms in Endogenous Depression. *The Journal of the Royal College of General Practitioners*, 15(4): 251–257.

13 Scapegoating and Splitting in Professional Teams

Scapegoating is a common problem for teams and exemplifies the defense mechanism called splitting. Scapegoating occurs when some team members view themselves as all good and chose one or two members as bad and worthy of abuse (DiGiuseppe & Perry, 2021). Scapegoating, splitting and self-glorification are part of a single process and indicate failure to integrate positive and negative qualities of self into a cohesive whole. Scapegoating suggests a simple primitive perception and is a commonplace phenomenon on teams where group regression is inevitable (Bion, 1968). Membership on any team promotes a childlike way of thinking. Splitting on teams typically occurs between starters and second stringers, with starters seeing themselves as good and the second stringers as bad. Being benched, being younger, smaller, being a rookie or getting injured invites membership into the so-called "bad" group.

James Grotstein (1985) suggested that the splitting defense first develops in infancy to help the baby to categorize complexity and to avoid feelings of confusion. However, according to Grotstein, the use of splitting is common in adults as well. Splitting is widely seen in today's increasingly complex postmodern culture and is evidenced by simplistic polarized thinking and the inability to engage in productive debate. In today's world, you are now either a liberal or a conservative, a democrat or a republican, from a red state or a blue state. There is no longer any in-between because the in-between place is too confusing, Splitting has become a worldwide psychological defense, is a part of postmodern life and there is by now ample evidence that we are witnessing a global regression in thinking (Baudrillard, 1994).

The starters on a team will project feelings of unworthiness, badness or weakness onto those on the bench who in turn introject these feelings of badness or inadequacy. Scapegoating is the expression of this dynamic.

68   Immature Defenses

> Projection in marriage: An exceedingly common dilemma in marriage is the way one partner will unconsciously project unresolved childhood affects into the partner. This results in the other partner internalizing or introjecting these feelings and in an uncanny way experiencing the mood of the partner's childhood. As an example, if one partner felt lonely and trapped as a child, over time, the other partner will experience a mood of loneliness and feelings of entrapment. This is a common example of the defenses of projection and introjection.

I will outline four cases which outline the common occurrence of splitting, projection and scapegoating on teams and how it can destroy seasons, team chemistry and even careers.

Case #1: *This case is a 17-year-old hockey player* who the mother described as "a gentle giant." He had symptoms of uncontrollable rage following minor mistakes made on the ice. He was bright, overweight, wore glasses, likable and somewhat schizoid in nature. His interests included engineering and mathematics and had no plans of playing college hockey despite the likely occurrence that he would receive a playing scholarship. He had been constantly bullied as a result of weight, having intellectual interests outside of hockey. The bullying eventually produced inner rage which he would occasionally express on the ice, which seemed to delight his teammates and he became "the enforcer" on the team. The team had scapegoated him into a marginalized role. He was rarely invited to team parties or get-togethers. His understandable rage at being scapegoated was worsened by the teams in encouraging him to "get mad" while playing since both he and they felt he was more dangerous when he played angry or the like "the hulk." The treatment of this patient focused on the dynamic of scapegoating which he had experienced over the last three years. The countertransference was very positive and it was easy for me to provide support for his value as we discussed his experiences of being scapegoated. When an athlete is helped to understand the group dynamic at play, it helps them to discard the negative introjections of badness and this goes a long way in helping them to improve self-image and let go of anger.

Case #2: *The Rookie Slump:* When this 16-year-old soccer player was moved up to the next level of competition, he suddenly lost confidence and fluidity. This is frequently referred to as the Rookie Slump. The process unfolds in the following manner. The rookie initially feels overwhelmed with uncertainty regarding his status on the new team. He begins to see his teammates and opponents as strong and good and begins to see himself as bad or weak. The athlete's play becomes hesitant and passive and little mistakes are perceived by the athlete as proof that he does not belong on the team. When this 16-year-old soccer player was invited onto a nationally ranked team, he suddenly looked like a different player, became afraid of being hit and was passive on the field. He was a defenseman and his role was to get close to the attackers, be annoying and physical. He has always been this way in the past, but upon entering this higher-level team, he suddenly developed this fear of being hurt and became passive, avoidant and timid. His regression into weakness and worry was a product of perceiving this team as "great, good and strong" and seeing himself as "poor, weak and fragile," thereby making him useless as a defenseman. Our work consisted of a discussion of this dramatic change of self-image and his feeling of suddenly being small, weak and fragile.

Case #3: *The is the case of a female Olympic-level gymnast* who was subjected to continuous splitting initiated by the coach of the national team and carried through by her teammates. This would be referred to as gaslighting and the teammates carried out the bidding of the coach. Upon graduating from college, this player joined the national team which was run by a coach who disliked her since the athlete had rejected his offer to join his college team. The coach's indignation led to him devaluing her performance and his attitude filtered into the teammates who acted out this attitude toward her. This is commonly referred to as enlisting "flying monkeys." The team would ridicule her body, her "tactless manner" and the way she dressed. She eventually introjected this devaluation and she became the scapegoat of the team, always wearing earphones and never interacting with teammates on bus trips to the stadium. This was in the era when female gymnast in America became a national craze with documentaries made about them as they performed in the Olympics. She was not included in these documentaries despite the fact that she was the second leading performer on the team. Based upon her willpower and talent, she somehow managed to withstand this kind of scapegoating and remained a dominant force in the world of gymnastics. She described her career as miserable and painful and she retired early. It took us many years to gain an understanding of the damage done to her by this team's act of splitting and negative projections.

Case #4: *Splitting Perpetuated by the Media:* Primitive splitting mechanisms are seen in the way media functions when it projects unrealistic glory on the chosen few and projects devaluation, neglect and lowness onto the rest of the field. I once had one of my celebrity patients tell me poignantly "Why doesn't the media understand that I'm just a regular person who happens to have one special skill. Why do they insist on expecting me to be an oracle on politics, virtue and wisdom?" This case I will now describe is a 26-year-old American tennis player who found his way to my office after struggling for years on the minor tennis circuits. Initially, as a youngster, he was ranked #2 in the nation in junior tennis and received much media attention from newspapers and television given his talent and good looks. He was labeled to the Andre Agassi. When a youngster of 14 is exposed to these kinds of projections, he happily introjects them, setting up an experience of expectation and pressure. Shortly after receiving an invitation to play in the U. S. Open at Flushing Meadow while only 15 years old, he began to have the serving yips which is a sign that his defenses were collapsing. This introjection of glorification and fame created self-consciousness every time he was in public. This led to feelings of chronic anxiety because in order to maintain this glorified status, he had to perform perfectly. Needless to say, the burden was too much for him as a teenager and he developed the yips. He managed to obtain a scholarship to a Division 1 college but languished on the mini circuits since then. The way the media functions is to split players into the best and the ranks. All athletes enjoy media attention and the fortunes that fame brings. However, the price and the burden of fame is great. In the film "Yesterday," an agent asks the musician who is about to become a star if he is willing "to drink from the poisoned chalice of fame and fortune." This is an accurate description of fame because it brings both good and bad. And invariably in the case of young athletes who obtain fame at a young age, the introject of being glorified often has a very toxic effect. I continue to work with this tennis player to help him to regain stability and sanity.

Scapegoating is a part of team dynamics and there is much more to be said about it. In this chapter, I merely wanted to introduce the way teams regress and resort to an overly simplistic way of viewing themselves and their teammates as either all good or all bad. The reality is that we are all a bit of both.

Key Points

- Scapegoating occurs on many teams and is a sign that the team is using a regressed childlike way of thinking.
- When a player is being scapegoated, it results in shame, anger and negative feelings.
- Scapegoating occurs with players who may be new, smaller, injured or different from the others.
- Splitting is seen worldwide with the prevalence of polarized thinking in politics.
- The so-called "Rookie Slump" can be explained with splitting where the rookie begins to feel less than the others.
- The media contributes to this form of simplistic thinking as they glorify a few star athletes and marginalize and neglect the rest.

> **Tips for Best Performance**
>
> If you find yourself being marginalized or scapegoated on a team, you are being subjected to unconscious and powerful group dynamics. Find yourself and trusted teammates so that you do not feel so alone. In addition, it may be wise to find a good sport psychologist to help you to rid yourself of this toxic state of mind. It is not your fault that this is happening.

Reflective Questions

- Define scapegoating.
- Why do you think scapegoating is common in teams?
- How does one defend against this toxic process if you are being scapegoated?

Exercise Drills for Best Performance

- Exercise #1: If you find yourself being marginalized or scapegoated on a team, realize you are not alone. The first thing to do is to be aware that it is happening, and when you see this pattern, you need to assert your feelings by saying things like "Stop this!" or "Find another scapegoat!".
- Exercise #2: Coaches need to be vigilant about scapegoating and address it in team meetings by exposing the ones who are doing the scapegoating.
- Exercise #3: Hazing is a form of scapegoating and ought to be monitored very closely by the coach so that it stays well within reason.
- Exercise #4: You have noticed a teammate has been scapegoated. As a result, their performance has suffered and they have become withdrawn from the rest of the team. Develop a strategy for resolving this situation. It might be helpful to create a script of how you would approach the topic, and what might be the most effective things to say to help your struggling teammate feel included again.

Recommended Reading

Wilfred Bion's Experiences In Groups. (1968) Routledge.

References

Baudrillard, J. (1994) *The Illusion of the End* (trans. C. Turner). Stanford University Press.

Bion, W. (1968) *Experiences in Groups*. Routledge.

DiGiuseppe, M. & Perry, J. (2021) The Hierarchy of Defense Mechanisms: Assessing Defensive Functioning with the Defense Mechanisms Rating Scales Q-Sort. *Frontiers in Psychology*, 12(7): 718440.

Grotstein, J. (1985) *Splitting and Projective Identification*. Jason Aronson.

14 Identification with the Aggressor as a Tool to Suppress Anxiety

Identification with the aggressor is a defense whereby one internalizes the characteristics of a more aggressive person. Internalizing the aggressive aspects of another gives one access to your own aggression and can be a useful way to inhibit anxiety in sports. Anna Freud felt that identification with the aggressor was one of the ego's most potent weapons in its dealings with anxiety (Freud, 1937).

I attempt to encourage identification with the aggressor with many anxious athletes by using it to reciprocally inhibit their anxiety. This device is similar to the behavioral technique of role modeling developed by Al Bandura in his social learning theory (Bandura, 1986). Role modeling or observational learning is where individuals learn to adopt new behaviors by observing others in the environment who act this way.

Wolpe's pioneering work in reciprocal inhibition paired the relaxation response with the anxiety-producing stimuli to reduce anxiety. He referred to this process as systematic desensitization (Wolpe, 1995). I believe that a more effective way to inhibit anxiety is to encourage aggression rather than relaxation. I refer to this technique at The Alpha Wolf Method (Ferraro, 2015). One teaches the athlete to suppress anxiety by identifying with an aggressive individual or even an aggressive animal. There are many successful athletes who can serve as aggressive role models (Mike Tyson, John McEnroe) as well as many predatory animals (lions or tigers). I will role model an aggressive attitude in the office with language, loudness and bodily postures like shoulders back, eye contact and other forms of dominance. We review the variety of ways one can show aggression such as snarling, grunting, spitting, acting arrogantly, cursing, all done to demonstrate strength and thus to directly inhibit the anxiety they are feeling which is disrupting their performance.

This strategy also borrows from Kelly's Personal Construct Theory which was a form of social learning and cognitive therapy. Kelly's Personal Construct Theory suggests that we all can change the way we act if we gain insight into how we define ourselves. He referred to this as constructive alternativism (Kelly, 1991). I expanded upon his insights into the world of the athlete by helping them to see that if they choose to adopt a tougher demeanor, they will not only inhibit anxiety but also become stronger and gain more confidence. All this sounds suspiciously behavioral in nature, but it is based upon the primitive defense of identification with the aggressor. Depending upon which sport we are dealing with, I will chose an athlete who is known to be aggressive. In baseball, we have Roger Clemens or Reggie Jackson, in football Joe Namath, in boxing Mike Tyson, in tennis there is McEnroe or Novak Djokovic and in golf Brooks Koepka. These are all very hostile, cocky and tough-minded athletes.

Tiger Woods and identification with the aggressor: A good example of a shy young athlete who was provided a tough role model to emulate is the case of Tiger Woods. As a child, Tiger was by nature shy, retiring and quiet. He wore glasses, stuttered and averted eye contact. His nickname was Urkel after the nerdy television character Steve Urkel who wore thick glasses and hiked up his pants with suspenders in the show "Family Matters." But over time, Tiger adopted the tough attitude of his father who was a Green Beret in the military and a trained killer. In addition to this kind of tough role modeling, before he left for a tournament when he was a youngster, Tiger Woods' mother would tell little Tiger to "go out there and kill them Tiger, kill them all." He was shown how to overcome his anxiety and shy temperament by identifying with his aggressive Green Beret dad and by permission from his mother to be aggressive.

Films often demonstrate the way the military employs identification with the aggressor to teach elite forces or Central Intelligence Agency operatives to become killers. The film series that began with "The Bourne identity" starring Matt Damon is a good example of this. The main character in these films is Jason Bourne who initially begins his life with a primary identity that is regular, mild and even meek. As he gets recruited and trained to be a killer, you see the way he dissociates fully from his main identity, and much of the plots of these films concern his efforts to return to his primary and kinder identity. But for our purposes, we want to explore the initial training and assimilation of a new more aggressive identity.

Case Study: #1: This patient was a female MMA boxer who came to me complaining that guilt was inhibiting her aggression in the ring and prevented her from embracing the "killer instinct." I had known of how Mike Tyson's sport psychologist was training Tyson to repeat certain aggressive phrases like "I will eat his children" to good effect so I introduced the topic of identifying with Tyson and adopting some of his highly aggressive attitudes and verbalizations as well. In addition to this, I made hypnotic tape where I induced a trance and then allowed her to visualize highly aggressive first-round knockouts. All of these methods worked well and this is a good example of directly teaching the defense of identification with the aggressor in order to inhibit his anxious guilt over hurting others.

Case Study: #2: This 12-year-old tennis player was brought to my office by his father who realized that his son was anxious and underperforming on the court. We discussed many elements from his past and efforts were made to resolve these traumas and instill insights into how his past was influencing his performance. One aspect of this process was our discussion of the way identification with the aggressor may help. His father was a gifted and highly intelligent entrepreneur and he created an excellent story for him to use while on the court. He suggested that his son see the opponent as an elephant and himself as a tiger about to pounce on the guy across the net and have him for dinner. This use of a predatory animal to identify with was helpful and allowed him to suppress some of his anxiety while playing.

The defense of identification with the aggressor can be used adjunctively to suppress anxiety, and despite it being considered a primitive defense, its use is of value for the anxious timid athlete.

Key Points

- Identification with the aggressor is a defense that can be used to suppress anxiety.
- Anna Freud suggested that identification with the aggressor was a potent tool to cope with anxiety.
- Teaching the use of aggression to inhibit anxiety is an extension of Wolpe's systematic desensitization, but rather than use relaxation to inhibit anxiety, I use aggression.
- Al Bandura's observational learning or role modeling can be used to help the athlete learn aggression.
- George Kelly's Personal Construct Theory is also useful in establishing on the field dominance by using a tough-guy demeanor.

Reflective Questions

- What does the term "fake it till you make it" mean and is there wisdom to this adage?
- Can you think of any tough-acting athletes that are good role models of strength and courage?
- How is aggressive behavior better than relaxation therapy if you want to suppress anxiety?

> **Tips for Best Performance**
>
> When faced with an athlete who is anxious, it is necessary to help them inhibit their anxiety by giving them permission to be aggressive, by role modeling aggression and by helping them to emulate a strong and aggressive athlete who plays their sport. This is a good way to overcome and inhibit anxiety.

Exercise Drills for Best Performance

- Exercise Drill #1: When faced with an athlete who is anxious, it is necessary to help them inhibit their anxiety by giving them permission to be aggressive, by role modeling aggression and by helping them to emulate a strong and aggressive athlete who plays their sport. This is a good way to overcome and inhibit anxiety. Pick a tough athlete who uses a tough-guy gaze, posture or attitude and practice this behavior over and over with the intention to use it throughout game day.

Recommended Reading

The Ego and The Mechanisms of Defense, Revised Edition (1937) Anna Freud, The International University Press.

References

Bandura, A. (1986) *Social Foundations of Thoughts and Action: A Social Cognitive Theory*. Prentice-Hall.
Ferraro, T. (2015) How to Become the Alpha Player on the Court. *New York Tennis Magazine*. Sept./Oct.
Freud, A. (1937) *The Ego and the Mechanisms of Defense* (trans. C. Baines). International Universities Press.
Kelly, G. (1991) *The Psychology of Personal Constructs: Vol. 1, Theory and Personality*. Routledge.
Wolpe, J. (1995) Reciprocal Inhibition: Major Agent of Behavior Change. In *Theories of Behavior Therapy, Exploring Behavior Change* (Eds. W. O'Donohue & L. Krasner). American Psychological Association, 23–58.

Part 2
The Neurotic Defenses

These defenses are referred to as compromise formations and are considered more mature and more adaptive than the previous mechanisms discussed.

15 Displacement of Anger into a Spouse

Displacement is the defense of redirecting a negative emotion or impulse from its original setting into a safer less cared for setting (McWilliams, 1994). Athletes who must deal with the many frustrations of competitive sports will frequently displace their game day frustrations onto the spouse when they arrive home. The use of this defense accounts for much of the domestic violence you read about in sports pages, and this displacement of frustrations also causes many divorces, when the abused spouse tires of taking unfair punishment. There are many athletes as well as coaches who use displacement to express rage. The University of Indiana basketball coach Bobby Knight would displace the rage he felt toward the referees by throwing chairs to vent his rage. Billy Martin, the New York Yankees coach, would displace his rage at an umpire by kicking dirt in the umpire's direction. And Heavyweight boxing champion Mike Tyson would displace the rage he is experiencing in the ring by abusing women. This behavior resulted in Tyson doing jail time.

The following case is a straightforward example of displacement by describing how an NHL player displaced his hockey frustrations onto his wife in the form of verbal abuse like cursing at her. I was originally contacted by the wife who felt that her husband, an NHL star, was depressed and underachieving. I began working with them both, and eventually, she shared with me his tendency to yell and curse at her after he returned home from an event where he did not perform as well as expected. This displacement was acted out verbally and by withdrawing into his bedroom and leaving her alone again despite the fact that he was home. This behavior is an example of displacement. The frustration of poor play was controlled for the most part while he played because on the professional level, overt misplaced aggression is not tolerated well by coaches, teammates or opponents. Sometimes, angry or inappropriate outbursts will be fined. The NFL fines players $25,000 for acting inappropriately after a touchdown is scored. PGA tour players who display anger by breaking a club will be fined $25,000. The NHL has similar rules. However, anger is often held in and ventilated and displaced at home toward the spouse.

Key Points

- Displacement is the defense of redirecting a recent or distant emotional state and placing it into another.
- Acts of domestic abuse in the world of sports are often best described as unconscious displacement of frustration from the sporting arena into the home.

Reflective Questions

- Define displacement and give two examples.
- Why is it so hard to express one's frustrations directly to the person that is causing the problem?
- What is a better way to handle one's anger?

Tips for Best Performance

Although it is difficult to observe, if you find yourself acting out frustration and tension after games by taking it out on a spouse or significant other, you need to do the following. If you feel the urge to lash out on a loved one, take a breath and ask yourself "Who am I actually mad at?" Eventually, you will come to realize you're actually mad at yourself and not the one you love. At that point, you need to learn to be more realistic about your performance and to learn to forgive yourself.

Exercise Drills for Best Performance

- Exercise Drill #1: It will be necessary to learn assertive skills in order to let go of the displacement defense. This takes time but if you practice being assertive in a safe easy setting, you will learn how to do so and you will see it is a far better defense.
- Exercise Drill #2: You have noticed yourself acting out and taking frustration out on your significant other after every bad match. Write down a list of techniques that can help calm down an athlete who is facing a loss. Once you have done this, try and see how you can make these

techniques long-term, so that the athlete is less likely to fall back into bad habits.

Recommended Reading

George Vaillant's "Adaptation to Life." Vaillant is a world expert on defense mechanisms and this easy-to-read book is a good way to understand the way defenses are used.

Reference

McWilliams, N. (1994) *Psychoanalytic Diagnosis, Understanding Personality Structures in the Clinical Setting.* The Guilford Press.

16 Repression and Reaction Formation in Asian Athletes

Repression is defined as the expelling of a feeling or thought from consciousness. This mechanism is the foundation upon which the theory of defenses was built (Freud, 1937). Reaction formation is the transformation of an unacceptable attitude, feeling or impulse into its opposite, such as smiling when angry. A good example of these two defenses was seen at the 2023 Open Championship in Hoylake, England. The young and ever-smiling South Korean Tom Kim was in his rental home after the second round of the event, caught his foot on the porch, fell down and dislocated his ankle. He was injured badly enough that he wanted to withdraw. His handlers then told him to suck it up, stop acting like a big baby and get ready for tomorrow's round. He listened and despite limping badly he smiled through the next two rounds and went on to nearly win the Open Championship. This is a good example of the use of both repression and reaction formation in action. Let us explore how these two defenses develop in the Asian athlete and how they characterize their athletic persona.

Asia has been influenced by the philosophy of Confucius who valued harmony, respect for others and subordinating oneself to the needs of family. Confucianism discourages the expression of feelings since it may infringe upon the harmony of others (Tang, 1997). In keeping with this philosophy, Asian children are taught to strictly control emotional expression. What is most forbidden is any direct expression of anger or aggression (Ferraro, 2002). Little to no interest is shown in how the child actually feels but rather the requirement is to fit in harmoniously with the family. Given this taboo against anger, the discouragement of emotional expression, the Asian child soon develops the defense of reaction formation or smiling if angry (Tang, 1997).

Let us explore the defenses of repression and reaction formation in the following.

Case Study #1: This is a case of a Japanese American nationally ranked female tennis player. This case demonstrates the three common defenses used by Asian athletes: repression, reaction formation and somatization.

82 The Neurotic Defenses

Repression is defined as expelling from conscious awareness any feelings considered unacceptable, reaction formation is managing unacceptable feelings by expressing them in antithetical form and somatization is the conversion of psychic derivatives into bodily symptoms (Meissner, 1985). This female athlete began playing tennis at the age of five, and by the age of eight, she was part of a nationally recognized elite tennis team. Her typical day was to rise at about 4:30 AM, where she ran for two miles and then was taken to the courts by her father and endure about 2 hours of training prior to school. After her morning workout, she was driven to school and attended classes like all the other elementary school kids. Immediately after school, she was again driven back to the courts by her mother where she practiced for about three more hours. She was then taken home, did her homework and went to bed only to start the same regiment the next day. On Saturdays, it was six hours of straight training and she was given off on Sundays. She repressed any and all feelings of fatigue, anger, complaint and pain and this went on for three years. Her demeanor and attitude through all of this was a reaction formation as she smiled, offered not a single complaint and secretly wished to at least be taken on a family vacation for a week. Vacations did not occur.

What did occur was a torn ACL in a national event when she was twelve. Her repression of anger, exhaustion and her reaction formation to smile through it all, led to this career-ending injury. The loss of her tennis career was met with relief as well as regret. And as she nursed her knee with physical therapy, she regressed into the use of somatization. She began to have a long and endless series of physical complaints which led to many medical doctor visits. Her somatic complaints included headaches, spotty, arm and leg pain, dizziness and blurred vision, none of which was found to be a disease process.

The development of these defenses was as follows. (1) She first used repression and reaction formation to avoid the awareness of fatigue and to transform any anger into smiles. This led to physical collapse in the form of a torn ACL. This was then followed by a regression into somatization to express her pain, anguish and depression. This process may be characteristic of the Asian athlete due to strict upbringing which reinforces compliance and cooperation and does not tolerate complaints.

Footbinding: A revealing and horrifying demonstration of stoic training, repression and pain tolerance in Asia is seen in the 1,000-year history of footbinding well documented by the Chinese scholar Wang Ping in her book "Aching for Beauty: Footbinding in China" (Ping, 2000). For a thousand years, Chinese mothers taught their daughters how to endure pain physically, emotionally and mentally. They

> bound the feet to beautify the daughter. But when feet are bound with ten feet of silk strips, the result leads to unbearable pain, broken bones in the feet, infections, odor, pus, sleepless nights, tears and extreme misery. And that had to be endured without complaint for years. This traumatic cultural phenomenon coupled with Confucianism's emphasis on harmony led to the establishment of these culture-wide traits.

The defenses of repression, reaction formation and somatization are central to child rearing in Asia (Tang, 1997) and one can observe these defenses in most Asian athletes in treatment. I believe these characteristics are the central reason that South Korean women dominate the LPGA today. These South Korean women are steadfast, unemotional, pain tolerant and seemingly oblivious to pressure. The Asian wave of golfers began with Se Ri Pak, Pearl Sinn and Birdie Kim and continues today with 38% of the LPGA made up of Asian women. On a book tour of South Korean, I recall talking to journalists in Seoul who lamented that nearly all of their young South Korean golfing stars would play for a few years and then leave the game entirely to return home, marry and have kids. It may be that the pain of repression and reaction formation eventually caught up to them all. The culture does not appear to embrace narcissism. The pull of fame was weak, whereas the mandate to have family and to escape from the torment of tournament pressure far outweighed both the need for money and fame.

When working with Asian athletes, I try to help them to understand how repression and reaction formation are defenses. We discuss the benefits and shortcomings produced by repression and reaction formation so the stress of competitive sports does not necessarily lead to exhaustion, overwork or pain or injury.

Key Points

- Repression is defined as the expelling of a feeling or thought from conscious awareness.
- Reaction formation is the transformation of an unacceptable attitude, feeling or impulse into its opposite.
- Asian children are raised in a culture which emphasizes self-control, family harmony and repression of negative emotions.
- Asian athletes tend to use repression to control pain and reaction formation to change anger into smiling.

84   The Neurotic Defenses

Reflective Questions

- Do you think that each area in the world has developed different ways of handling anxiety and if so, how?
- How do you think the Asian mindset manages to repress pain and do you think this mindset can be taught to athletes from other nations?
- Do you think centuries of footbinding and the pain it produced has had an impact on the Asian mind, and if so, how?

Tips for Best Performance

Although repression is effective in automatically expelling both negative feelings and thought, the chronic use of this defense can be unhealthy. To repress feelings of pain or fatigue can push the body too far and illness, burnout and even injury can result. If you find that your performance is flat and no improvement is being shown, it may be that you are using repression and you are overworked. This means it's time for a break. Rest and recovery are important parts of excellent performance.

Exercise Drills for Best Performance

- Although repression is effective in automatically expelling negative feelings and thought, the chronic use of this defense can be unhealthy. To repress feelings of pain or fatigue can push the body too far which can cause illness, burnout and even injury. If you find that your performance is flat and no improvement is being shown, it may be that you are repressing pain and fatigue and that you are overworked. Rest and recovery are an important part of excellent performance. The best drill for this is to discuss your workout and competitive regiment with your trainer or coach in order to establish a rest and recovery schedule on a daily, weekly and monthly basis.
- Exercise 1#. Design a guidance leaflet for athletes outlining how to describe and prevent burnout. Consider the role of rest and recovery in your message.

Recommended Reading

Wang Ping's award-winning book "Aching for Beauty; Footbinding in China."

References

Ferraro, T. (2002) Aggression Among Athletes: An Asian versus American Comparison. *Athletic Insight*, 1(1): 16–22.

Freud, A. (1937) *The Ego and the Mechanisms of Defense* (trans. C. Baines). International Universities Press.

Meissner, W. (1985) Theories of Personality and Psychopathology; Classical Psychoanalysis. In *Comprehensive Textbook of Psychiatry. IV*, Vol. 1 (Eds. H. Kaplan & B. Sadock). Williams and Wilkin, 337–418.

Ping, W. (2000) *Aching for Beauty, Footbinding in China*. Random House.

Tang, N. (1997) Psychoanalytic Psychotherapy with Chinese Americans. In *Working with Asian Americans, A Guide of Clinicians* (Ed. E. Lee). Guilford Press, 323–341.

17 Overcompensation
Turning Inferiority into Superiority in a LPGA Golfer

Alfred Adler defined the defense of overcompensation as an effort to cope with feelings of inferiority by becoming highly skilled in another area (Adler, 1956). This defense enables one to ward off feelings of weakness by overcompensating through hard work, thus establishing a feeling of superiority. Adler based his psychological theory of defense on his knowledge of the biology of organ inferiority. This biological premise states that when the body inherits an inferior organ, it will eventually compensate for this inferiority by developing exceptional superiority through another organ. Albert Einstein had a small left cortex so his right cortex grew in size and accounts for why he became a mathematical genius. Overcompensation was seen with Olympic track star Wilma Rudolph, who had polio and wore a brace throughout childhood, yet she went on to win the 1960 Olympic gold medal in the 100 yard dash in Rome, Italy.

In Goertzel and Goertzel's classic text "Cradles of Eminence," the lives of 300 famous men and women were studied and the Goertzels's discovered that a common factor in these cases of greatness was being born into poverty or having a physical infirmity which gave them an underlying drive to overcome this inferiority (Goertzel & Goertzel, 2004). Other examples of overcompensation are seen with Helen Keller who was blind, Gandhi who was slight and frail and Teddy Roosevelt who was sickly and asthmatic as a child. The Goertzels's concluded that greatness stems from experiencing great loss and suffering as children which motivates one to strive ahead no matter what the obstacles.

Case Study #1: Thanks to participation in a documentary on extreme sports I had a chance to study someone who overcame adversity and made it to the top of the heap. This was a professional hand cyclist who has won major marathons. She was once a wheelchair bound invalid who was born with primary immune deficiency disease and Ehlers-Danlos syndrome. As an adult, she had a serious car accident which entailed multiple surgeries to save her leg. This athlete's obsessive drive pushed her to achieve victories in these excruciating endurance races which required extraordinary pain tolerance. Adler's theory of overcompensation explains this drive. This athlete reacted to her early childhood infirmities by refusing the sick role of being a weak invalid. She turned her weakness into strength.

Case Study #2: Overcompensation was seen in a world class golfer I worked with who had a hearing deficiency in childhood and was unable to process or understand language spoken to him. In addition, he was born into poverty, had never met his mother and his father was overworked, strict and unloving. As he grew into his teen years, he was short, overweight and wore glasses. However, all of the adversity he experienced, including hearing loss, poverty, lack of adequate parenting and shortness of stature gave him extreme motivation to overcome this sense of inferiority. His body developed superior visual capacity to compensate for his hearing loss and he was able to read greens and observe what each golf hole demanded of him. He went on to achieve world class status and, at one point, was top six in the world ranking in golf. His drive to excel was best explained by his need to overcompensate for his sense of inferiority.

Case Study #3: This athlete played on the tennis tour and climbed her way to the top between the years 2020 and 2022. She was raised by a demanding father who never gave her compliments and she grew up in the shadow of an older sister who was very beautiful and which produced feelings of ugliness in my patient. Over time, she overcompensated for her sense of inferiority and ugliness by concentrating on tennis night and day and eventually she made it into the top 30 ranking worldwide. Overcompensation does indeed produce higher than average performance based upon hard work and singular focus. The weakness of this defense is that the underlying dynamics of inferiority strives for expression in some way and is like a shadow or cloud that never leaves the athlete. This athlete's sense of inferiority finally reemerged during a Wimbledon semifinals. She was about to close out the match and proceeded to double fault her way to a loss. The year after that, she lost all form and lost her playing privileges.

Why did her overcompensation defense break down? Alfred Adler's theory of overcompensation states that childhood feelings of inferiority lead the person to adapt to these feelings of inadequacy by overcompensating. The patient's history showed she was the second born and her older sister was both beautiful and social. My patient grew up in the shadow of her older sister and felt inferior, ugly and awkward in comparison. In addition, the patient's father was demanding and difficult to please. These circumstances produced the overcompensation but her over striving to gain approval was endless and led to fatigue, frustration and the eventual breakdown of the defense. What emerges was a flood of self-doubt, negativity and anxiety. The course of her therapy was to help her to understand both her overdriven overcompensation and her underlying sense of inferiority based upon her family dynamics. She still works with me to understand this and to achieve a more reasonable belief system. All neurotic and primitive defenses are helpful to some degree but over time have limited value and can backfire.

> A personal story: A good example of overcompensation is seen in me. I had an older brother who was extremely gifted academically. Ever since childhood, I have thought of myself as slow, dull witted, not too bright, somewhat delayed intellectually and saddled with a poor memory. This sense of inferiority fueled my academic growth, and since my mid-twenties, I have been reading, learning, writing and publishing. I am a good example of overcompensation. So, if you learn things in this book, you can thank my exceptionally gifted older brother which caused me to study, read and write day and night for the last 60 years.

Key Points

- Adler's theory of overcompensation is elegant and simple. It means that if you grew up feeling small and weak, you will often overcompensate for this by striving for superiority in some area of your life.
- Many athletes use the defense of overcompensation to get beyond a sense of inferiority. The black star tennis players, Venus and Serena Williams, grew up on the mean streets of Los Angeles in poverty and amidst violence. However, thanks to parental support, they overcame their sense of inferiority and dominated the previously all white world of tennis.
- It should be noted that like all defenses, they are compromise positions at best and take much energy to maintain. Over time, they do break down and so it pays to understand how one's history dictates the defenses we establish so that they can be improved upon.

Reflective Questions

- Do you think athletes use overcompensation to overcome past insecurities? Give one example.
- What would be an example of an inferior ability that needs to be compensated for.
- Although it is obvious that overcompensation provides motivational fuel to many athletes. What is the drawback of overcompensation?

Tips for Best Performance

If you grew up in the shadow of an older sibling and harsh parent which made you feel inferior, it is likely you are trying to overcompensate by achieving great things in one area of life. This is positive but make sure you take time to realize that you have come far and give yourself reminders that you have successfully overcome your childhood sense of inferiority. As Freud said "Where id was, there ego shall be" (Freud, 1933). This simple statement means that unconscious feelings from your past remain inside of you and so you need to learn to give these feelings words and gain insight which then helps you to get free of them.

Exercise Drills for Best Performance

If you grew up in the shadow of an older sibling who made you feel inferior, it is likely you are trying to overcompensate by achieving great things in one area of life. This is positive but make sure you take time to realize that you have come far and give yourself reminders that you have successfully overcome your childhood sense of inferiority. As Freud said "Where id was, there ego shall be" (Freud, 1933). This means that one needs to understand one's feelings of weakness and then realize one has outgrown ones "inferiority." A good drill is to make a list of your most recent accomplishments, put these up on your wall and read them each morning.

Recommended Viewing

The Academy Award winning film "King Richard" starring Will Smith is about the life of the Williams sisters. The extreme hardship experienced by the Williams family is shown in detail and it is easy to see how the family used overcompensation to go beyond the circumstances they grew up with.

References

Adler, A. (1956) *The Individual Psychology of Alfred Adler*. Basic Books.
Freud, S. (1933) New Introductory Lectures on Psycho-Analysis. In *The Standard Edition of the Complete Works of Sigmund Freud* (trans. J. Strachey). Hogarth Press, 4699.
Goertzel, V. & Goertzel, M. (2004) *Cradles of Eminence*. 2nd edition. Great Potential Press.

18 Doubting in Athletes and the Intellectualization Defense

Intellectualization is defined as the control of emotions or impulses with excessive thinking about them without experiencing the emotions. It enables the athlete to avoid anxiety but at a cost of spontaneity, fluidity, creativity and power. Athletes will often refer to this as "overthinking" but will have little insight as to what to do about it. The defenses of undoing, rationalization and magical thinking are defenses that fall under the category of intellectualization defenses (Vaillant, 1992). Hockey players, golfers, pitchers, tennis players and basketball players have told me they often "overthink" too much. In this chapter, I will present three cases that reflect the use of these kinds of defenses.

Intellectualization is used by obsessive compulsive athletes and Leon Salzman calls obsessives as stricken with the disease of doubt (Salzmann, 1985). When an athlete has doubt about the outcome of a shot or a pitch, he will hesitate. They hesitate because they are not willing to face the possibility of failing and fear the self-attack that will follow. Doubting leads to hesitation which leads to underperforming, and this is a common problem for the obsessive compulsive overly intellectual athlete.

Case Study #1: This Division 1 football basketball player came to me with depression and anxiety of long-standing duration. He complained that he was hesitating before throwing in his position as quarterback. His hesitation on the field lowered his overall performance and he was failing to live up to the coaches' expectation for him. He was currently considered a second-string player. He was a bright student who had parents who were highly educated professionals who were both critical of him. Despite his obvious talent, he was always worried about his performance and was afraid to throw interceptions. As we talked about his fear of failing and how this produced hesitation, he was able to engage in a discussion to his harsh self-criticism and where it was derived from. He was perfectionistic and obsessive and needed to have control of all things, which prompted him to scan the field in doubt rather than just throw the football. This a relatively new case and thus far the insights into his harsh perfectionistic attitudes have helped. He came with doubt and an intellectual worried approach to performance, and over time, we will continue to outline this defense and why he is so worried about failure. Insights about this dynamic will eventually allow him to internalize a more acceptable and more realistic view of performance outcomes, and in turn, he will be less intellective and doubting and more free. It should be noted that it was not positive self-talk and encouragement to be free or to be forging that affected change but rather the insights into his defense of doubt and hesitation and his fear of making a mistake.

Case Study #2: The next case is an amateur golfer who was a bright, well-educated professional engineer who was a devoted golfer playing with a six handicap. Although this is a respectable enough handicap, this athlete invested considerable time and money into improving his game. But despite all of his efforts, including lessons, hiring a personal trainer, having the best equipment and playing at least three times per week, he was at a plateau and came to me in the hope that he could learn why. He was a highly verbal man who used an intellectual, mechanical approach to golf. His numerous swing thoughts were slowing his swing, cost him distance and gave it a mechanical appearance. He was thinking his way through the swing as opposed to allowing his natural ability to reign free. Overthinking is remarkably common in bright athletes who use it to undo the feelings of anxiety about the possibility of failure in each shot. His career as an engineer was spent analyzing and thinking in details which benefited him in that setting but not in golf. I encouraged the athlete to discuss and explore in detail the feelings of aggression and fear of failure he had underneath this defense, and we endeavored to help him accept failure as an inevitable part of every sport. Over time, this approach helped him to learn to enjoy the game and to swing freer.

Case Study #3: Rationalization as another aspect of intellectualization: Rationalization is the justification of behavior by using incorrect logic. I work with a tennis player who uses rationalization. He is a player who tends to break the rules by making poor calls against opponents. At times, this behavior is spotted by fans or the media, and when confronted after the match by umpires or opponents, he will typically justify or rationalize the behavior in a way that sounds relatively persuasive but most understand it to be a lie. He uses this defense so well that he personally is convinced of its truth and he is able to complete matches without guilt and without a loss of focus. This is a case which demonstrates the ability of a defense to work effectively enough to shut out guilt or anxiety. In that sense, it works, but it also cost him many millions in lost endorsement dollars from corporations who demand excellence in performance, looks and ethics.

The Neurotic Defenses

Key Points

- Intellectualization is a defense of controlling feelings with excessive thinking.
- Athletes will refer to this tendency as "overthinking"' and it causes a lack of fluidity and loss of creativity.
- This tendency to intellectualize is shown with hesitation and doubt about the outcome of a shot.
- Rationalization and magical thinking fall under this category and they can be helpful in avoiding guilt but will exact a cost in reputation.

Reflective Questions

- Explain how avoidance is related to overthinking.
- The slogan by Nike "Just do it" refers to the need to act rather than think things to death. Why is it that some people defend against failure by overthinking so much?
- What are athletes trying to avoid by overthinking?
- What do you think the athlete needs to do in order to have the courage to act?

Tips for Best Performance

Rationalization of the justification of behavior that others consider to be wrong should not be addressed until after the tournament since this defense helps the athlete to maintain focus without undo guilt.

Exercise Drills for Best Performance

- In order to get into the habit of taking risks rather than avoiding things, do the following drill. Every day, choose one thing that you have been avoiding. Bite the bullet, take the plunge and then assess how things turned out. Also be sure to compliment yourself for doing so.
- Athletes get into the habit of avoiding, becoming passive on the field because they fear making mistakes. To manage this problem, get into the habit of consciously forgiving yourself when you make a mistake. Remember "To err is human, to forgive is divine."

Recommended Reading

D.H. Lawrence's 1923 "Studies in Classic American Literature," Penguin Books.

References

Lawrence, D.H. (1923) *Studies in Classic American Literature*. Penguin Books.
Salzman, L. (1985) *Treatment of the Obsessive Personality*. Jason Aronson.
Vaillant, G. (1992) *Ego Mechanisms of Defense; A Guide for Clinicians and Researchers*. American Psychiatric Press.

19 The Undoing Defense
Why Athletes Choke

Undoing is the defense mechanism where a person cancels out some behavior perceived to be threatening, wrong or guilt inducing. The process of doing and then undoing describes the self-defeat process often seen in sports. When a golfer performs well on the front nine only to undo it on the back nine with a bad score. Many years ago, Mark Cannizzaro of the *New York Post* was doing a column about my sport psychology work and I invited him to my club to show him how I work. We played together and I applied some standard focusing and visualization techniques which allowed him to shoot a 39 on the front nine, the best nine holes of his career. He then promptly undid this by shooting a 51 on the back, thereby demonstrating the defense of undoing. Perhaps, he felt he did not deserve it nor did he feel he was capable of duplicating his front nine score.

Sigmund Freud was the first to discuss the way success produces shame and must be undone. In his classic essay "Those Wrecked by Success" (Freud, 1916), he wrote:

> Some people fall ill precisely when a deeply rooted and long cherished wish has come to fulfillment. It seems then as though they were not able to tolerate this happiness. For there can be no question that there is a causal connection between their success and their falling ill.

Freud felt many patients have an inability to perceive their own achievements, felt that success was too good to be true and managed to undo their success in a variety of ways. Anna Freud described the defense of doing/undoing with obsessives compulsives who repeat a behavior, anorexics who eat a full meal and throw it up or children who build a castle of blocks only to knock them down again (Freud, 1937).

Felix Deutsch (1959) was a pioneer in the field of psychosomatic disorders and following up on Sigmund Freud's essay "Those Wrecked by Success." Deutsch outlined the way physical illness is often produced by any number of mysterious unconscious dynamics, including guilt and distorted self-images. By now, there is a vast literature on psychosomatic disorders which readily and regularly convert mental and emotional problems into the body. People get headaches when angry, diarrhea or nausea when anxious. It takes no leap of logic to therefore assume that athletes undo victory by choking based upon any number of unconscious problems, including guilt, low self-image or feelings of inadequacy.

The behaviorist Leon Festinger's theory of cognitive dissonance is an elegant extension of the undoing defense and describes how a person's self-belief about who they are clashes with what they have just achieved. This will result in an undoing of the achievement to regain a feeling of equilibrium and identity stability.

There are many examples of this doing-undoing defense in the world of sports. The way that Tiger Woods destroyed his reputation as one of the world's most admired athletes may be a good example of this defense. He managed to undo a lifetime of achievement, status and financial success through sexual misbehavior. By recklessly engaging in sex with prostitutes, and getting caught, he single-handedly "wrecked his success" and undid his fame, and his bank account.

I will give two examples of athletes I have worked with who have used undoing as a defense and how it damaged them both on the playing field and off.

Case #1: This is a case of a middle-aged amateur golfer who had a tendency to choke when coming down the stretch in tournaments. It became so obvious that he had this pattern than one of his caddies, witnessing him implode on the 16th hole and failing to finish off an event remarked "here we go again." This golfer had a repetitive dream where he would hit a wonderful shot onto green from 230 yards away only to watch as the ball first came close to the hole and then inexplicably roll off the green and back to his feet. This dream expressed his undoing defense. And in golf tournaments, he would play well for about 2/3's of the round only to undo his success by bogeying in. Our job in this case was to help him to understand the meaning of his pattern of self-defeat on the course. He said continued success during a round of golf meant that he felt increasing anxiety. This produced a pattern in him of avoiding this experience by beating himself to the punch and getting away from the stress through self-defeat. And in the case, self-defeat was more attractive than experiencing the anxiety felt as one strived for victory. His anxiety was so intense that he had unconsciously decided to undo his success by failing.

Case #2: The second case showing the defense of undoing is seen in a professional golfer I work with who was stuck on the Korn Ferry Tour, the minor leagues of golf. Like most professional athletes, he had demonstrated considerable talent but he was saddled with anxiety. He expressed his anxiety by worrying, doubting his ability and experiencing nausea, a

96   The Neurotic Defenses

> Choking: Choking is a term for the athlete that undoes success in the end and exemplifies Anna Freud's comments about the vomiting anorexic who would first eat food and then throw it up. And the case of the athlete, he first eats victory, swallows some of it and then chokes it up. Golfers sometimes use the phrase "throwing up on myself" when describing a round where they gave up their lead. Undoing to avoid the pressure of success is also nicely explained by Bibring (1953) who suggests that the feeling of helpless anxiety that occurs as one nears success is so problematic that many chose to avoid all risk. I will go into detail about this theory in Chapter 39 ("Depression used as Defense by Athletes.")

choking feeling in his throat and vomiting before tournaments, all classic signs of "undoing" as we discussed in the last case. He was seen twice weekly and he was conscientious in keeping his appointments, despite his busy schedule. We spend weeks working through his anxieties, and as his earnings rose, he neared the point of qualifying for the PGA. On the eve of his next tournament, he was staying in a rental home, and as he was walking down the stairs in his socks, he fell and seriously hurt his back. Needless to say, this produced a layoff of many weeks and he did not qualify for the PGA. As Freud said, accidents are usually dictated by unconscious motives. In this case, we can see clearly that he once again had undone his success out of the fear that the next step would be intense, stressful and perhaps unmanageable. He defended against this upcoming opportunity by an injury that sidelined him for an extended period. His unconscious defense of undoing shielded him from experiencing the next phase of pressure which was sure to be felt on tour. Teeing it up against Rory McIlroy or Dustin Johnson is daunting.

Athletes have a host of ways of unconsciously protecting themselves from pressure and potential failure that is felt at the next level of the game. They can unconsciously fail before they get to the 18th green as we saw in the golfer. They can get an injury to remove themselves from competition at the next level. As Freud described in "Those Wrecked by Success," the next level of achievement is only available to those strong enough and confident enough to withstand the pressure.

In the Oscar winning film "Yesterday," directed by Danny Boyle, the main character was on the threshold of success, and before he was thrust into the spotlight, his agent sat him down in her opulent living room and she directed him to say "I want to drink from the poison chalice of fame and fortune." He hesitated and she repeated, "You must tell me you want to drink from the poison chalice of fame and fortune." He finally was able

The Undoing Defense: Why Athletes Choke   97

to say it. The reason that scene was so compelling was because it dealt with the inevitable pressure of success and fame, something athletes face every time they step onto the playing field and every time they have a chance to get to the next level. They must be ready to walk through Jung's liminal space and be ready to face the fiercer competition. Most fear success because with it comes anxiety and the real possibility of public humiliation and failure. Success is accompanied by risk, pressure and pain. The undoing defense is the way many athletes opt out of success and protect themselves.

Key Points

- The undoing defense occurs when a person cancels out or undoes some behavior perceived to be threatening, wrong or guilt inducing.
- Examples of the undoing defense are seen when athletes choke which demonstrates the inability to take in and swallow success.
- Freud wrote "Those Wrecked by Success" which was a character type with guilt.
- Tiger Woods is a good example to the way an athlete can undo all the success and fame built up over a career.

Reflective Questions

- Why do you think athletes choke?
- As victory approaches and the pressure mounts, some athletes shy away from the big moment. Why?
- Self-belief seems to be important in coping with pressure. Why?

Tips for Best Performance

If you find yourself giving up leads, it might be because you are using the undoing defense. Ask yourself if you think you deserve to win and think about why you may be feeling undeserving of success.

Exercise Drills for Best Performance

A good drill is to make a conscious effort to build esteem by listing your past sports accomplishments. Then, you need to anticipate the pressure because it will come as victory nears. Rehearse the self-belief you will recite to yourself when under pressure. The late great singer Sammy Davis

Jr. would kiss his ring before going on stage and say to himself "You're a star, you're a star, you're a star."

Recommended Viewing

The film "Yesterday" directed by Danny Boyle. This film is about the pressures and challenges of success and how one musician comes to terms with it. Pay special attention to the scene in Malibu with the agent and the singer.

References

Bibring, E. (1953) The Mechanism of Depression. In *Affective Disorders, Psychoanalytic Contributions to Their Study* (Ed. P. Greenacre). International Universities Press, 13–48.

Deutsch, F. (1959) On the Formation of the Conversion Symptom. In *On the Mysterious Leap from the Mind to the Body: A Study on the Theory of Conversion*. Ed. F. Deutsch International Universities Press, 59–74.

Freud, S. (1916) Those Wrecked by Success. In *Some Character-Types Met with in Psycho-Analytic Work, Standard Edition of the Complete Works of Sigmund Freud* (trans. J. Strachey). Hogarth Press.

Freud, A. (1937) *The Ego and the Mechanisms of Defense* (trans. C. Baines). International Universities Press.

20 Isolation of Affect Defense in Athletes

Isolation is a defense where emotion is detached from an idea by rendering the affect unconscious and thereby transforming the thought into something bland and emotionally flat. This defense is of great benefit to the elite athlete like pitchers, golfers and quarterbacks because they must remain poised, self-possessed and cool as they try to make a downhill left to right breaking putt to win a tournament or throw a breaking curve ball against Aaron Judge to win the World Series. The ability to screen out or isolate emotions is one of the keys to winning in sports. This ability is difficult to learn and it may be a primary reason that athletes seek psychological help. Freud's investigation of defenses focused primarily on repression and isolation. He defined isolation as the person's ability to create a gap between an unpleasant cognition and feelings that accompany them by minimizing associative connections with other thoughts so that the threatening cognitions are remembered less often and is less likely to affect awareness (Freud, 1961).

The following case study is a professional tennis player I have treated for the last three years. His childhood was marked by traumatic physical abuse, at the hands of an alcoholic father. As a teenager, if the patient failed to win a match, the father would physically pummel and hit him in the parking lot before they went home. His mother was neglectful and of little help in sheltering him for this abuse. He slowly developed the defense of isolation which allowed him to detach from his emotions in a dissociative way in order to withstand the beating. The ability to isolate affect turned out to be of enormous benefit when playing tennis.

He referred to this ability as compartmentalization. I would watch him win match after match while in majors, and when I asked him if he felt any anxiety during the final points, he would say "No, not really." This skill is invaluable in any game which regularly requires you to stay emotionally calm but cognitively clear while under duress. It is also curious to me that he was able to use the exact term for the defense he was using. Compartmentalization is the precise term that theorists use when defining

The Neurotic Defenses

the defense of isolation. This defense is very effective for the competitive athlete and thus no intervention is needed when they have use of it. But for the athletes who have not developed this defense, there will be guides in the Tips for Best Performance section. The reason that drugs are so ineffective for athletes is because calming medications like a tranquilizer or a beta blocker blur cognitive acuity, the skill so necessary in all sports.

> The isolation defense used by Korean golfers: Korean woman currently dominate the LPGA and the question frequently asked is why. Their cool demeanor was expressed in a controversial statement made by LPGA star Jan Stepheson who remarked that the Asian women all seemed so cold, unfriendly and aloof. However, when one interacts with them, they are far from cold and in fact are consistently kind, charming and friendly. However, there on-course demeanor during tournaments, which was what Stephenson was referring to, is uniformly cool, calm and unflappable. Another good example of the Asian mind is Tiger Woods whose mother was Thai. His ability to separate his emotions from the reality of the moment is remarkable. I can recall standing next to him on the putting green at Shinnecock Hills Golf Club prior to the U.S. Open. We were alone on the green and his ability to remain isolated and focused was so keen that it remains the only time in my life that I experienced the sensation of being invisible and non-existent. It was as if I, along with the thousands of adoring fans that gazed at him, did not even exist. Such was the power of his defense of isolation. The question that still remains is how does the Asian mind develop in this way. The Asian culture had Buddhist roots which emphasize stoicism. Their languages have far fewer words for pain than in the English language. I go into greater detail about these Asians traits in Chapter 41 (Cultural Differences in the Way Athletes Use Defenses) but suffice it to say that Buddhism's emphasis on stoicism and the repression of emotion, along with the 1,000-year-old practice of foot binding and the more recent Cultural Revolution, have combined to establish the defense of isolation of affect in its citizens.

However, based upon the case study above, who was an American tennis player, it is apparent that the use of the isolation defense comes from a childhood under the influence of a physically abusive or demanding parents. The well-known aphorism "no pain, no gain" sadly applies in this case. This tennis player made great gains in his career, thanks to his ability

Isolation of Affect Defense in Athletes

to isolate his emotion from the reality of the moment. However, it was the pain of abuse that enabled him to establish this ability.

Key Points

- Isolation is the ability to emotionally detach from an idea placed by your emotions into the unconscious.
- Isolation and repression were Freud's central concern when studying defenses.
- Many Asian golfers seem to employ the defense of isolation.

Reflective Questions

- Define the defense of compartmentalization.
- During the impeachment hearings of President Clinton, despite the stress he was under, he showed an ability to ignore the stress and carry on his duties as president. Explain how he may have used compartmentalization to do this.
- Why do you think Asian athletes have this ability to compartmentalize emotions and remain calm under pressure.

Tips for Best Performance

In order to establish the ability to isolate your thoughts from your emotions when under pressure, one needs to "reset" your mind by establishing a gap between thoughts. When you become aware of getting overwhelmed with emotions, as a pitcher, a tennis player, or golfer, say "STOP!" take a deep breath and focus your eyes on the target you are hitting to. This will give you time to separate your appropriate thoughts from those emotional thoughts which are producing the anxiety.

Exercise Drills for Best Performance

- Exercise Drill #1: To isolate your thoughts from your emotions, you need to "reset" the mind by establishing a gap between thoughts. When you become aware of getting overwhelmed with anxious emotions, say "STOP!" take a deep breath and focus your eyes on the target you are hitting toward. This will give you time to separate your appropriate thoughts from those emotional ones which are producing the anxiety. This is called pre-shot routine in golf and golfers do this every time

they are about to hit a shot. No matter what sport you play, you ought to have a pre-shot routine which helps you to compartmentalize your thoughts from extraneous emotions.
- Exercise Drill #2: Develop an assessment and monitoring plan to manage athletes dealing with compartmentalization. What advice would you give? What activities would you recommend the athletes try out in their own training?

Recommended Viewing

Tiger: The Authorized DVD Collection.

Reference

Freud, S. (1961) *The Standard Edition of the Complete Works of Sigmund Freud* (vol. 20). Hogarth Press.

21 Dissociation in Sports

Dissociation is the temporary but drastic modification of identity used to avoid pain, anxiety or emotional distress. This neurotic defense is often associated with post-traumatic stress or an abuse history; however, some athletes use this defense to cope with their pain, exhaustion or stress. Dissociation and depersonalization develop in children based upon repeated experiences of traumas (Terr, 1999). Children dissociate to escape from feelings of helplessness, pain or repetitive shock (Terr, 1999, p. 74).

Some controversy surrounds the mechanism of dissociation. Is this defense developed because of the traumatic experiences they have faced or is this a pre-existing personality trait (Horowitz, et al. 1999). Dissociation and hypnotizability are found in those with higher-than-average IQs which suggests that this defense is partly related to genetic endowment and partly due to the experience of chronic abuse or pain (Spiegel et al., 1988). I have treated endurance athletes like long-distance swimmers or runners who use the dissociation defense to deal with pain and exhaustion.

The cases reviewed in this chapter will include a nationally ranked long-distance swimmer and a golfer who used dissociation to manage pain, fear or exhaustion. The defense of dissociation enables strong pain tolerance which athlete's need to manage the many grueling moments they face as they compete. Both the benefits and the drawbacks of this defense will be outlined.

Case #1: The long-distance swimmer who dissociated before races. Endurance athletes like marathoners enter into a dissociated almost hypnotic fugue-like states, enabling them to cope with pain. This swimmer came to me for a consultation because he was concerned about his mental health. He was an affable, gentle, soft-spoken athlete who was a nationally ranked swimmer who had been awarded a full scholarship to a Division I college and wanted to prepare himself for his college experience. His history revealed that he was raised by an abusive father who would have physical fights with him and would verbally abuse him on a daily basis. When I asked him of any swimming-related fears, he mentioned that he was afraid

104   *The Neurotic Defenses*

that someday he might drown. When I asked him why a talented swimmer would fear drowning, he remarked:

> I turn into a different person during a race and call myself 'The Animal'. When I race I have only one pace whether it's an 800 meter race or a 1,600-meter race. I go all out every lap. And recently I passed out while swimming.

This level of extreme effort to the point of passing out indicates not only outstanding pain tolerance but also the tendency to enter a dissociative state. When I asked him to elaborate on his nickname "The Animal," he said "You wouldn't want to be near me before any race. I actually become a different person altogether. I get nasty, aggressive, hostile." This is evidence that he temporarily dissociated into a different person. These sudden changes in demeanor are a less severe version of multiple personality disorder and are not accompanied by amnesia for the altered states of being.

Case #2: This case is a 19-year-old golfer who came to me with the putting yips. He had been to multiple orthopedic surgeons and neurologists, but they did not find anything neurologically or physically wrong. He came to my office as a last resort. History revealed that he was an accomplished golfer who had won a number of AJGI events around the nation but the putting yips were of great concern. When he was putting, the club would inadvertently jerk in his hands at impact. His family history revealed that his stepfather was a sinister, abusive and frightening figure. The patient told me that recently he had won a tournament in California and returned home to New Jersey the next day. It was snowing and the father insisted he hit shots rather than rest after this grueling tournament. Another incident between father and son again reveals the extreme terror and anxiety the son felt. One day while playing golf together, he hit a bad shot and was so terrified that his father would scream at him that he dropped his golf bag and ran home. This and many other incidents revealed that the father was abusive. After only a few interactions I had with the father, I told my patient that if I was ever forced to interact with the father again, I would terminate the case. An example of how this athlete dissociated was seen in his fitness workouts. I was concerned that he was working out too much and I asked him to describe his gym routines. He said that all of his routines were done until exhaustion or vomiting set in. This form of extreme punishing of the body and pain tolerance is evidence of dissociation. As mentioned above, Lenore Terr's work on childhood trauma suggested that children who must deal with extremes of physical suffering undergo character reorganization and employ self-hypnosis or dissociation. I see evidence that some athletes and especially endurance athletes or those with abuse histories develop dissociative, self-hypnotic techniques that allow them to tolerate pain.

Ronald Fairbairn was one of the founders of the object relation school of psychology and believed that children dissociated away from the internalized images of bad parents and over time these dissociated aspects became part of what he referred to as internal saboteurs. These dissociated internal saboteurs would eventually emerge later in life and produce self-defeat (Fairbairn, 1952). Fairbairn and most other object-relations theorists rely on the defense of dissociation to explain what occurs when a child is raised abusively. They suggest that dissociation or vertical splitting is used as a defense rather than repression. This theory provides us with proof that one does not need a life-threatening trauma to develop dissociation. A history of abuse and the choice of any endurance sport is enough to have one develop and use this defense.

Key Points

- Dissociation is defined as the ability to temporarily modify one's identity in order to avoid pain, anxiety or extreme stress.
- Endurance athletes will sometimes use dissociation in order to cope with pain.
- The work of Ronald Fairbairn and other object-relations theorists believe that dissociation, rather than repression, is the primary defense used by people.

Reflective Questions

- As you drive to work each day or as you are reading this sentence, you are in a dissociated state. Explain.
- How do hypnotists get people to dissociate so quickly?
- Multiple personality disorder is an extreme use of dissociation based upon a history of severe abuse. Describe a movie you have seen that has a character with multiple personality.

Exercise Drills for Best Performance

- Exercise Drill #1: Although it is difficult to create the defense of dissociation in adults, one method that approximates it is to learn how to self-hypnotize. To do this, you need to take a few deep breaths. As you inhale and exhale, let your mind become aware of the sensation of your lungs expanding and contracting. This is called the induction phase of hypnosis. After this you choose to focus on any physical movement that relates to your sport. For a golfer, it may be your swing tempo or the target; for a runner, it may be the movement of your legs as they move up and down. When you learn to focus on the rhythm of your body or on an external target, you are briefly entering a dissociative state.

- Exercise Drill #2: To learn the value of dissociation, do the following. Stand on one leg and try to maintain your balance. See how long you can do it. Then, do it once again, but this time focus your eyes on a single spot on the wall, stand on one leg and see how long you do it this time. You can maintain balance much easier by focusing on a single spot which means that you are visually dissociating away from leg imbalance by looking at the spot. This is a brief hypnotic state.

Tips for Best Performance

Although it is difficult to create the defense of dissociation in adults, one method that approximates it is to learn how to self-hypnotize. To do this, you need to take a few deep breaths. As you inhale and exhale, let your mind become aware of the sensation of your lungs expanding and contracting. This is called the induction phase of hypnosis. After this, you choose to focus on any physical movement that relates to your sport. For a golfer, it may be your swing tempo or a target; for a runner, it may be the movement of your legs as they move up and down. And when you learn to focus on your body in this way, you are learning self-hypnosis.

Recommended Reading

Roy Udolf's Handbook of Hypnosis for Professionals. Second Edition.

References

Fairbairn, W.D. (1952) *Psychoanalytic Studies of the Personality*. Routledge.

Horowtiz, M., Wilner, N., Kaktreider, N., & Alvarez, W. (1999) Signs and Symptoms of Posttraumatic Stress Disroder. In *Essential Papers on Posttraumatic Stress Disorder* (Ed. M. Horowitz). New York University Press, 22–40.

Spiegel, P. Hunt, T. & Dondershine, H. E. (1988) Dissociation and hypnotizability in posttraumatic stress disorder. *The Amerinca Journal of Psychiatry*. 144 (3): 301–305.

Terr, L. (1999) Childhood Traumas: An Outline and Overview. In *Essential Papers on Posttraumatic Stress Disorder* (Ed. M. Horowitz). New York University Press, 61–81.

22 Reaction Formation
The Problem of Being Mr. Nice Guy

Reaction formation is a defense where one manages an unacceptable impulse by permitting the expression of its opposite (Nemiah, 1978). When someone is mad but instead they smile, this is reaction formation. Reaction formation can be either a defense against aggression, dependency or passivity. We will discuss these three types in this chapter. If an athlete feels uncomfortable about being aggressive, his will to win is replaced by kindness, empathy, pity or sympathy. When they use this defense, the athlete loses power and is prone to choking.

Case Study #1: *Reaction formation against aggression*. This is a case of reaction formation that developed into a character trait in a young golfer with the chipping yips. He was a personable athlete, well-liked, successful in school but was prone to the yips around the green. His yips were severe enough to put his future golfing career in doubt. He had a fairly easy-going pleasant personality, smiled often and our initial discussions focused on the causes of his yips and the embarrassment it was producing. I used standard relaxation therapy, positive self-talk and distraction tools at the outset of our work. These tools had no discernible impact on his yips. Prior to the yips, he was a dominant high school golfer and it was expected that he would be recruited and play in college. However, his chipping yips became so bad that he was now entertaining the thought of quitting golf altogether. He was the oldest of five children and his father was a dominating and intimidating figure who was extremely successful. The patient told me of memories of rough and tumble play with the father while growing up, but these playful interactions at times turned into more serious fighting. These repetitive interactions with the father appeared to have instilled a fear of aggression in this athlete and produced a reaction formation against aggression. This eventually translated into a generalized character trait which converted aggression into friendly passive weak non-intimidating demeanor (Reich, 1945). Whenever his aggression and will power were called upon in a match or in social settings, he would suppress his anger and replace it with smiles and a weak demeanor. Eventually, he developed panic attacks as well as the yips on the golf course. He had a series of dreams about running away from a big older man with a gun. One does not have to be a highly trained psychoanalyst to see that this athlete was desperately trying to manage his aggressive urges by running away from them. The result was an inability to muster strength and focus when he needed it most.

> Kawaii syndrome in Japan: An example of reaction formation on a nationwide scale is seen with the kawaii syndrome in Japan. It has been said that the trauma of Hiroshima and Nagasaki has created a tendency of the Japanese people to present themselves as cuddly and defenseless in order to avoid any future provocation which could lead to another nuclear holocaust. Japanese artist Takashi Murakami curated the art show "Little Boy" (referring to the H-bomb dropped on Hiroshima) in order to develop this idea. He supported many artists from Japanese otaku or "Geek culture" to demonstrate this theme. The kawaii syndrome is a national reaction formation to avoiding the threat of future atomic annihilation. The power of cuddly non-threatening cuteness has been used by global fashion houses. Murakami's kawaii-based art was noticed by Marc Jacobs, the creative force in charge of the Louis Vuitton brand who invited Murakami to play around with the LV logo in 2003. They have been profiting from this collaboration ever since. The global presence of Hello Kitty, the pretty Japanese kitten with no mouth is currently franchised to over 15,000 products worldwide. The fact that the Hello Kitty has no mouth is a good example of reaction formation. No matter what inner feelings going on, they are not to be expressed (Ferraro, 2016).

Case Study #2: *Reaction formation against passivity*. This type of reaction formation is frequently seen in men who doubt their masculinity and who cannot tolerate any conscious awareness of feminine or homosexual tendencies (Sachs, 1984). These men will appear as gruff, macho and tough and will seek tasks that require strength, physical prowess, courage and pain tolerance. Long-distance runners, marathoners, Ironman participants and bodybuilders may be seen using this defense. Wilhem Reich's concept of character armor fits this defense well. Reich suggests that both defenses and neurosis form a character armor around the patient which they use defensively as protection (Reich, 1945). The case I will present now is a 40-year-old dentist who in his spare time lifts weights. He will rise every day to work out before going to his office and he has been competing in local and regional Mr. Olympia events. He tells me he likes to stay trim and fit and takes great pride in having all of his clothes tailor made. His childhood history was of interest. His uncle was a closet homosexual and molested him during childhood. The assault on his young male identity produced a powerful defense against homosexual tendencies and he thereafter embarked on a lifestyle of pain tolerance, endurance training and toughness all in an unconscious effort to ward off any hint of femininity or homosexual feelings. His reaction formation of compulsive bodybuilding has made him an exemplar of fortitude and strength for all who see him. His driven disciplined lifestyle has unwittingly converted his fear of homosexuality, weakness and vulnerability into strength. As insight into this defense was gained, I have also encouraged him to ease up and to enjoy his life more and turn away from his Spartan-like lifestyle. Charles Barkley was famous for his quote that "athletes are not role models." This point is debatable. This patient was an example that athletes are role models of power and fortitude and this ought to be a source of personal pride. However, the only way that the patient can come to this realization of pride and purpose is by gaining insight into his fixated use of reaction formation. The tragedy of rigid defenses is that they can produce wonderful results, but the patient is often the only one who cannot appreciate these achievements. In this case, the patient was on a treadmill of effort, was unable to ease up and this resulted in arm and chest injuries during weight training.

Case Study #3: *Reaction formation against dependency*. Reaction formation against dependency is seen in athletes who resist any dependency or guidance from coaches or sport therapists. They are seen as super independent, stubborn and uncoachable. Many athletes are loathe to become dependent because it implies weakness and they fear that dependency may lead to disappointment if they rely on others. The character Willie "Steamin" Beamon in the football film "Any Given Sunday" was a good example of a standoffish, pseudo-independent uncoachable athlete. The character was played by Jamie Foxx, and there was a scene in the airplane where he was seated alone with earphones on and his coach, played by Al Pacino, approached him to try to connect. Pacino was unsuccessful. These types of athletes are very self-sufficient, hardworking and dislike vacations.

The case I will discuss here is one I did not treat directly. I was asked to be a consultant in a film about the ultra-endurance cyclist. I introduced this case in Chapter 18 (Overcompensation). This female athlete is a professional handcyclist and about to take part in the Race Across America which was a 930-mile race from California to Colorado over mountains and through deserts. The film maker, Crispin Kerr-Dineen, wanted some insight into her motivational system and so I was consulted and became a part of the film. The athlete's history revealed she was born with a severe primary immunodeficiency disease and Ehlers-Danlos syndrome (EDS), and throughout childhood, she was repeatedly told by doctors that due to her weak body and fragile joints, she could not participate in sports. Then, in 2006, she had a serious car accident which led to multiple leg surgeries and she was told she would never walk again. This prompted her to say enough with the bad news and she began to train for a half marathon. Her EDS worsened and she had spinal cord problems, and so, under the advice or her physical therapist, took to hand cycling instead. Since then, she has been competing successfully in many endurance races, won both the NY and Boston marathon in her division and has become world famous and a heroic symbol of human courage and tenacity. This is a good example of the reaction formation defense. She refused to accept the diagnosis of being a cripple or weak and instead chose a pathway to glory and became a role model for all the disabled in the world. Here, we observe the slow maturation of defenses from neurotic mid-level reaction formation to altruism, one of mankind's highest states of being.

Key Points

- Reaction formation is the management of an unacceptable impulse by converting it into its opposite.
- Reaction formation against aggression is always counterproductive for athletes who need to tap into their aggression in order to win.
- Reaction formation against passivity is seen in men who react to fears of femininity or homosexuality by becoming rough and tough.
- Reaction formation against dependency is seen in injured or ill athletes or athletes who distrust others, and these athletes all act if they don't need others.
- Reaction formation can change into a prosocial altruistic defense with the help of insight and support.

Reflective Questions

- Why do you think it's best for an athlete to express their anger or aggression?
- Why do people smile when they are mad?
- Why do nice guys finish last?

Tips of Best Performance

If you see that you tend to choke and lose focus or aggression in the final moments of play, you may be using reaction formation or fear your own power. The best way to change this fear of aggression is to allow yourself to be tough, tell yourself that no one dies if you get strong. The defense of reaction formation or fear of aggression gets converted into a personality characteristic of smiling friendliness. This trait may have its benefits in business or at home but it often works against you when you are trying to win.

Exercise Drills for Best Performance

Exercise Drill #1: The defense of reaction formation or fear of aggression gets converted into a personality characteristic of smiling friendliness. This trait may have its benefits in business or at home, but it often works against you when you are trying to win. If you tend to lose aggression in the final moments of play or when your opponent is intimidating, you may have conflicts about your own aggression and anger. The best way to overcome this fear is to allow yourself to be tough, tell yourself that no one dies if you get strong. Use a role model who shows toughness and emulate them.

Further Reading or Viewing

- The film "Forrest Gump" to observe reaction formation against dependency.
- The film "Any Given Sunday" to observe reaction formation against dependency.
- Superflat art by Takashi Murakami to observe in Japanese the national reaction formation known as kawaii syndrome.

References

Ferraro, T. (2016) The Japanese Power of Cute: How Hello Kitty, Pikachu, and Kaikai Have Become a Global Force. *A List Magazine*. Fall.

Nemiah, J. (1978) The Dynamic Bases of Psychopathology. In *The Harvard Guide to Modern Psychiatry* (Ed. A. Nicholi). The Belknap Press of Harvard University Press, 147–172.

Reich, W. (1945) *Character Analysis*. Simon and Schuster.

Sachs, M. (1984) A Psychoanalytic Perspective on Running. In *Running as Therapy, An Integrated Approach* (Eds. M. Sachs & G. Buffone). University of Nebraska Press, 101–111.

23 The Yips in Golf as an Example of Repression

Repression is defined as the withholding from awareness a feeling or desire that the athlete feels uncomfortable with. The unconscious use of repression is the cause of much self-defeat in sports. When athletes suddenly lose their fluidity, their aggression and their focus as they near victory, this may be due to the process of repression. This kind of self-defeat is familiar to athletes, coaches and sport psychologists and the standard psychological intervention is to apply anxiety control interventions such as relaxation therapy, deep breathing, autogenics, meditation, rational emotive therapy (RET) or distraction techniques to relax and refocus the athlete. These interventions have proven to be remarkably unsuccessful (Dahal, 2018; Gardner & Moore, 2006). Often when an athlete "spits-the-bit" or backs off the lead, they may be unconsciously repressing their aggression, due to an unconscious fear of retaliation, guilt about overpowering the opponent or the anxiety that a win will produce a separation. Under these unconscious influences, athletes repress their powers at the last minute.

Case Study: This Irish American PGA player demonstrated the use of repression, a defense that derailed his entire career. In this PGA event in Texas, there were 150 players invited to play in the first two rounds and then the low 65 and ties are invited into the third and fourth rounds where they earn money. Any player who fails to make the cut does not earn money and considers the week a failure. This player had lost his playing status and, in this event, he was not only trying to earn money but also to regain his playing status. During round one, he played well, made a few birdies and was 1 under par after one round. This placed him at the cut line which meant he would have to do the same the next day for him to qualify for weekend play. But on his first nine of round two, he played tentatively, made no birdies, three bogies, and by the middle of the back nine, he knew he would have to birdie in to make the cut. He proceeded to birdie the last three holes but failed to make the cut by one. So, how does one go about explaining what happened in round two? Why did he lose form, play tight and without aggression on that front nine and then suddenly seem to wake up and make birdies only to fail by one shot? It seems reasonable to suggest that something changed on day two. He seemed to block his aggression, lose focus and his sense of urgency. He became less dominant and let the field pass him by. When it became apparent that he would not make the cut, he allowed himself to wake up and birdied in. He had grabbed defeat out of the jaws of victory. What could be so taboo about winning? Consciously, he wanted this win but he managed to repress his aggression, power and focus. Any use of anxiety reduction techniques in cases like this invariably makes things worse since repression has already weakened the athlete.

We must go back a few years to find the cause for this. Years ago, at the peak of his career when he had full playing privileges, he was in contention in the Masters and a bizarre incident occurred. During round three, he felt that he may have moved his ball slightly in the pine needles. He finished the round but was so plagued by guilt he asked an official later that night about this and he was reassured that he had done nothing wrong and that the ruling was based on the player's determination alone. This guilt reaction perpetuated itself and he began to ruminate which caused fatigue and anxiety. When I asked him to associate with the guilt he felt during the Masters, he said that his father was a postal worker and had once casually remarked to the patient that the son made more money in a week than he did in a year. In addition, the players, three younger siblings and all of his friends at home were all middle-class blue-collar workers. As the player transcended all of his siblings, his father and his friends, he had an increasing sense of separation from them all. His ruminating guilt over a non-infraction at the Masters was nothing more than the inevitable straw that broke the camel's back. His unconscious guilt over separating from all of his loved ones had produced this obsessive rumination which slowly derailed his career. The more recent choking in the second round in Texas may have been derived from the initial guilt. Guilt over domination of others accounts for his flat second round performance. Repression of his talent related to guilt over outdoing his siblings and friends.

What does one do to help the repressive tendency that leads to choking like this? One must work through the repression and the underlying guilt that causes it. And following this insight, one must help the athlete to find another method to cope with anxiety as victory approaches. Harry Stack Sullivan (1954) suggested that insight is good enough because this prompts the patient to engage in a trial-and-error quest to replace old neurotic patterns with new healthier ones. However, it seems reasonable to offer some advice in this way to help replace the largely ineffective defense of repression with another more effective one. Following the gaining of insight, I will often help the athlete work through the insight by pointing them toward more mature defenses such as humor, identification with the aggressor or other defenses. Identification with the aggressor can be prompted by

114 The Neurotic Defenses

pointing out aggressive role models in sports like Tiger Woods for golfers. You can prompt them to think about using humor by citing examples like Lee "The Merry Mex" Trevino.

Freud (1915) wrote that the essence of repression lies simply in turning something away and keeping it at a distance. This is exactly what happens to the athlete who represses their power and aggression. They are unconsciously turning away from victory by repressing their will to win. And often upon realizing what is happening during the round, they wake up, come back to form but it is usually too late. The job of the sport psychologist is to help the athlete who is using repression to wake up faster. Athletes may unconsciously fear dominating others or that victory may cause separation from loved ones. These dynamics often have their roots in earlier relationships with either mother, father, sibling or friends. This is a complex process but the reality is that there are no short cuts. Medication cannot provide an athlete with the ability to manage their fears of winning. Self-help tips are not strong enough to deal with these internal conflicts that lay in the unconscious. The only reasonable answer is to help the athlete, in this case a golfer, gain insight into internal and hidden conflicts about winning and success.

Key Points

- Repression is defined as the defense where an athlete withholds from awareness the desire to win.
- Self-help tips are of little use when unconscious repression is being used by the athlete.
- When a player seems to lose form as victory approaches, they may be using repression which cuts off their power and aggressive desires.

Reflective Questions

- How would you define repression?
- Why would an athlete repress their desire to win?
- How are the yips related to repression?

Tips for Best Performance

If you find yourself backing off of leads and playing tentatively or without focus, it may be because you are repressing your power. A good way to begin to overcome this is to choose an aggressive athlete to emulate. This may help you to overcome your repressive tendencies. In addition, insight into the reasons for your fears of winning is needed as well.

Exercise Drills for Best Performance

If you find yourself backing off leads and playing tentatively, it may be because you are repressing your power and your will to win. It may be useful to do two things. Firstly, ask yourself what is it you have against winning. It may be you have a hard time with pressure or a past memory will emerge as you ponder this question. A good way to begin to overcome this is to then begin to anticipate the pressure that you will inevitably feel as you near victory (see Chapter 28 for a full explanation of anticipation). As you make a plan about this, you will need to establish a brief mantra which will remind you to stay focused or to believe in yourself. This will help you to remain calm.

Recommended Reading

Harry Stack Sullivan's The Psychiatric Interview.

References

Dalal, F. (2018) *CBT: The Cognitive Behavioural Tsunami*. Routledge.
Freud, S. (1915) Repression. In *The Standard Edition of the Complete Works of Sigmund Freud*. Vol. 14 (ed. And trans. Strachey. Hogarth, 141–158.
Gardner, F. & Moore, Z. (2006) *Clinical Sport Psychology*. Human Kinetics.
Sullivan, H.S. (1954) *The Psychiatric Interview*. W. W. Norton and Company.

Part 3
The Mature Defenses

The higher-level defenses maximize function and gratification and are considered optimal adaptations to stress by allowing for the conscious awareness of feelings as well as thoughts. In addition, the mature defenses require less energy to maintain thereby providing the athlete access to more energy to perform with.

24 Counterphobia or Why Athletes Compete

Counterphobia is the process of facing fear rather than fleeing from it. Counterphobia is demonstrated by NASCAR drivers who have chosen a career where they face fear every day. Freud felt that athletic trophies serve as a reminder that the person has faced a grave risk and survived. He suggested that there are many types of thrill-seeking behaviors that are counterphobic in nature, including traveling to foreign lands, going on adventures, rock climbing and going to amusement parks. When one successfully faces down these dangers, the athlete is able to conclude that they are brave and not afraid or weak (Freud, 1961). The theme of counterphobia as defense was later developed by Helene Deutsch (1926), suggesting that the pleasure of the sporting situation was partially derived from the opportunity to face childhood fears in order to master and control them. Otto Fenichel considered counterphobia a "flight into reality" and a courageous effort to master repressed childhood fears (Fenichel, 1933), and more recently, Nancy Mc Williams includes counterphobias among the higher-order acting out defenses where a person seeks frightening situations in order to convert a sense of helplessness into agency (McWilliams, 1994).

Competition provides the chance to face the fearful opponent, the frightening father, the older sibling. Sports presents the question "Can I face the big guy, not blink and triumph?" The use of the sport metaphor "sudden death playoff" hints at this unsettling underlying dynamic. In this chapter, we will explore the way a professional rock climber repeatedly faced death every time he climbed.

Case Study: Rock climbing was put on the map with the Academy Award winning 2018 documentary "Free Solo" about Alex Honnold's solo climb up the 3,000-foot face of El Capitan in Yosemite National Park. He did this without ropes. I received a call from another professional rock climber's mother pleading for help because of his compulsive need to take risks. This athlete was a world class sponsored rock climber. He was raised in a home with a physically abusive alcoholic father. When he was a teenager, this athlete was already showing world class talent, but if he did poorly in competition, his father would attack him physically on the way home from the event. These attacks occurred frequently and with such intensity that one day they had a serious physical fight in the living room of the house when the athlete was 19. Following that accident, he left home and has not seen his parents in seven years.

The athlete went on to a stellar career in rock climbing and he was known as a workaholic and great competitor until one day when he fell and was nearly paralyzed. This provided him some motivation about his career choice.

So, how is one to understand these features of my patient's career? He compulsively competed, took risks and faced death on a daily basis. Why? I think the only way to explain this is to understand it as an entirely unconscious counterphobic defense which reenacted his frightening childhood at the hands of a violent alcoholic father. He was now driven to recreate these scenarios by picking fights with mother nature herself, a formidable foe.

The work we did consisted of establishing a working alliance, providing support and offering a chance to him to ventilate his frustrations, his sadness over the injury, his history and his fears. I think there was a tentative identification with me in order to soften his harsh super ego and trust me enough to discuss his violent upbringing. I think Nancy McWilliams is right in categorizing counterphobia as a higher-order defense in that it allowed the patient to remain at a distance from his more frightening childhood memories and at the same time constantly overcome them slowly with these discussions. As Freud said, all of his trophies, his ribbons and his fame serve as an unconscious reminder that he was able to face up to the monster that was his father and survive the abuse. And insight into this dynamic freed him from the compulsion that he must do it over and over again. Outcomes in therapy allows the athlete to make reasoned choices about things rather than be trapped in a compulsive death-defying cycle.

Key Points

- Counterphobia is the defense of facing your worst childhood fears and surviving them.
- Freud felt that trophies serve to remind the athlete that they faced grave danger and survived.
- Fenichel felt that counterphobias were a courageous effort to face our fears.
- The compulsive embrace of danger is seen in this rock climber who faced down gravity and mother nature herself and lived to talk about it.

Reflective Questions

- Give three examples of people you know who like to face their fears.
- Do you think anyone in uniformed services (police or fireman) has chosen their profession to face down their fears?
- Is the sports term "sudden death" alluding to the athletes need to face death and conquer it?

Exercise Drills for Best Performance

- Competitive athletes who face their fear need to realize how courageous they are. The trophy is a symbol that an athlete has proved their courage. Make sure you put your trophies on display and spend time talking about your wins with those who care about you. This helps one to recognize the feat you have accomplished so that in the future you may have less fear the next time you face off with an opponent.
- But if you find that you are burned out, injury prone and unhappy with your performance, no matter how well you're doing, this may be a sign that you are blindly creating a childhood scenario that you are trapped in. It is best to be aware of what motivates you to play so that you gain a measure of control over it. If you are unhappy with your sport and injury prone, ask yourself if you are being unconsciously driven by the ghost of past fears.
- For practitioner: It is wise to help the athlete to go back and discuss the source of their anxieties in order to help them gain more control of their motivations.

Tips for Best Performance

- To face one's fear is a commendable endeavor. Any competitive athlete has been able to face their fears by winning trophies. Make sure you put your trophies on display and spend time talking about your wins with those who care about you. This helps one to recognize the feat you have accomplished so that in the future you may have less fear the next time you face off with an opponent.
- But if you find that you are burned out, injury prone and unhappy with your performance, no matter how well you're doing, this may be a sign that you are blindly creating a childhood scenario that you are not aware of. It is best to be aware of what motivates you to play so that you gain a measure of control over it. If you are unhappy with your sport and injury prone, ask yourself if you are being unconsciously driven by the ghost of past fears.

> - For practitioner: It is a truism that the athlete's drive and compulsion to compete is based upon childhood fears and anxieties. If you see that the athlete is prone to exhaustion or injury, it may be due to his or her unconscious need to face and overcome childhood anxiety. It is wise to help them to go back and discuss the source of their anxieties in order to help them gain more control of their motivations.

Recommended Viewing

- The film "Fearless" starring Jeff Bridges is about surviving a plane crash and how the survivor adopts a counterphobic attitude toward death.
- The Academy Award winning 2018 documentary "Free Solo" about Alex Honnold's climb up the 3,000-foot face of El Capitan in Yosemite National Park.
- Michael Mann's 2023 film "Ferrari," starring Adam Driver. Focusing on Italian entrepreneur Enzo Ferrari as he prepares his racing team for the Mille Miglia, the film looks at F1 drivers' relationships with speeding, adrenaline and the fear of death.

References

Deutsch, H. (1926) Contributions to the Psychology of Sport. *International Journal of Psycho-Analysis*, 7: 223–227.

Fenichel, O. (1933) The Counter-Phobic Attitude. *International Journal of Psycho-Analysis*, XIV: 263–274.

Freud, S. (1961) *Civilization and Its Discontents* (trans. J. Stachey). W. W. Norton and Company.

McWilliams, N. (1994) *Psychoanalytic Diagnosis: Understanding Personality Structure in the Clinical Process*. Guilford Press.

25 The Value of Self-Observation for Athletes

Self-observation represents the capacity to realistically see oneself without distortion, grandiosity or devaluation (Di Giuseppe & Perry, 2021). This defense may be the sine quo non of mental health, and is often referred to as the observing ego in psychoanalysis. This highly adaptive defense prevents undo reactivity to minor events and provides the ability to understand oneself, one's capacities, how others actually perceive you as well as to accept the vagaries of life. A good example of the value of this defense was expressed by Woody Allen when asked what he learned after 25 years of four times per week psychoanalysis. He paused and quipped "I no longer ruminate." This may sound like an offhanded sarcastic remark, but it actually reveals a valuable truth. When one has acquired the defense of self-observation, you are able to accept minor occurrences and setbacks for what they are or when one possesses an observing ego. One could argue that his 25 years of psychoanalysis was a waste of time and money, but how many other directors do you know who were able to write, direct, produce and star in films every year since 1966. Allen has won Academy Awards and his films like "Annie Hall" have even set fashion trends. His prodigious productivity is most certainly in part due to his having worked on himself psychologically which has given him the ability to self-observe and gain distance from his anxiety rather than endlessly ruminate about things. He is able to use all of his energy to create rather than to worry.

The case study in this chapter is an ex-hockey player who played on the Division 1 level. After college, he entered the workforce and gained employment with a global accounting firm. He was bright, perfectionistic and obsessional in nature and well suited for his role in the company. When we began working together, he was still in college and playing on an academic and athletic scholarship. He felt stressed both in the locker room and on the ice. He grew up in a family with a father who was critical and neglectful. As a young player, he suffered by feeling like an outsider in a jock culture because of his intelligence and specialized interests in mathematics. He overcompensated for this sense of inferiority by overtrying which led to

DOI: 10.4324/9781003436270-29

exhaustion and depletion. Coaching input felt to him like a criticism reminiscent of how his father interacted with him. All of this led to such unhappiness and stress that he gave up his athletic career and focused on his academic work during his last year in college. After graduating, he entered the world of the corporation with an atmosphere urging the employees to work long hours. He tended to misinterpret statements made to him as being negative and began to worry that he may be fired despite his excellence and his work ethics. At that point, he still failed to have the ability to fully self-observe himself in a realistic way. We have worked weekly for about five years, and only recently, he has begun to adjust his misperception and gain some distance on his anxiety and reduce his rumination and needless worry. He is slowly acquiring the adaptive defense of self-observation, the skill I hope for with the patient. We work to help them face up to and resolve past pains and present distortions and to finally arrive at a place where they can use all of their energy and talent to produce good for themselves and the world.

He has slowly learned to pause, observe the situation and to convert anxiety into a calmer more reasonable state of mind. The acquisition of this defense is one of the primary objectives of all therapy and helps the athlete to stabilize mood, normalize behavior, prevent any acting out, avoid overwork and depression. That is the ultimate goal of therapy, and it occurs only if and when the defense of self-observation is acquired.

Key Points

- Self-observation is the highly adaptive defense or capacity to see oneself realistically, without distortion, with grandiosity or self-attack.
- To acquire this defense means you no longer are apt to ruminate or worry obsessively.
- When the athlete learns this defense, they have far more energy to play their sport.
- It takes an extended period to achieve this ability to pause, not to worry, to forgive oneself and refocus and it is the ultimate goal of therapy.

Reflective Questions

- To be self-aware, have an observing ego and self-accepting is the sine qua non of mental health. Why do you think it's so difficult to achieve self-acceptance?
- Why do you think people ruminate, worry and exaggerate their concerns?
- To be self-observant means to have the ability to stay in the moment. Explain.

Exercise Drills for Best Performance

- Drill #1: After any mistake on the field, get into the habit of PAUSING and saying "Let it go. Worry does not help."
- Drill #2: Get into the habit of saying "Good enough is good enough."

> **Tips for Best Performance**
>
> After any and all mistakes you experience on the field, get into the habit of PAUSING, FORGIVING YOUR SELF AND REFOCUSING.

Recommended Viewing

The 1999 film "For Love of the Game" starring Kevin Costner as a Major League Baseball pitcher who uses his ability to pause and refocus in order to pitch a perfect game.

Reference

Di Giuseppe, M. & Perry, J. (2021) The Hierarchy of Defense Mechanisms: Assessing Defensive Functioning with the Defense Mechanisms Rating Scales Q-Sort. *Frontiers in Psychology*, 12:1–23.

26 Altruistic Surrender in Sports or Why Athletes Give Away Leads

Altruism is defined as coping with stress by meeting the needs of others. Acts of charity, volunteerism or heroic sacrifice are examples of altruism. In Victor Frankl's book about surviving the concentration camps, he referred to altruism as lifesaving and the key to finding meaning in life (Frankl, 1959). The defense of altruism has a long and conflicted history in psychoanalysis. Anna Freud referred to this as "altruistic surrender" or masochism. She felt that devotional giving to another was a denial of one's life instincts and thus was highly problematic (Freud, 1966). Winnicott's false self-concept is an extension of Anna Freud's concerns about giving too much. The false self describes the character trait serving the needs of others and not yourself (Winnicott, 1971). However, not all theorists have felt that altruism was a form of masochism. George Vaillant thought of altruism as one of the highest forms of defense by managing emotional needs through dedication to others (Vaillant, 1992). The trait of altruism is reinforced by religions such as Judaism and Catholicism which suggests one love to neighbor as oneself.

> Dog ownership as an example of altruism: If one analyzes dog ownership, one easily sees that it's an expression of altruism. The domesticated dog is essentially dependent upon its master for food and shelter. The owner will selflessly tend to the animal's needs by giving it shelter, feeding it, grooming it, taking it for walks and taking it to the veterinarian, all of which cost money. In America, 66% of homes have at least one pet which indicates how common our altruistic urges are (Megna, 2024).

In sports, altruism can also be a mixed blessing. It can lead to positive team chemistry and a valuable asset, producing team chemistry. However, too much altruistic compassion and concern for one's opponent can lead to self-defeat and giving away leads. The first case will demonstrate altruistic surrender and demonstrates Anna Freud's assessment that altruism is a form of masochism. The second case will be more aligned with Valliant's view of altruism as a high-level and more positive defense by exploring the heroic efforts of a famous handcyclist who willingly gave her all and served as a positive role model for all who were handicapped.

Case Study #1 of altruistic surrender: This professional tennis player has been seen twice weekly for over five years. At the outset of our work, it was clear that in many tournaments he gave away leads to his opponents as a nicely wrapped present and handed them victory. Over time, we used insights and a host of techniques to help him to resist this compulsion to be an altruistic gift giver by handing over wins. Our work appeared to be effective, and evidence of altruistic surrender by giving away leads began to diminish over the years. However, this trait of altruistic surrender runs deep and tends to resist removal. One day recently, he called in a distressed state. He had a new business and had hired a "friend" who was a general contractor to manage the construction of this multi-million-dollar project. The progress of the construction was slow and over budget and my patient began to make phone calls to the manufacturers who the contractor was dealing with. It became evident that his "friend," the general contractor, was taking the money he had given to him to begin the project ($4,000,000) and had pocketed it. Within a few weeks of investigating, it became evident that this was true and his friend was a sociopath. When I asked him why he had hired this guy as a contractor on such a big project, he said "I knew he was down and out and I wanted to do him a favor by offering him this big opportunity." Thus, we see how this altruistic surrender was alive and well, although no longer evident during his competitive play. This example of giving too much, what Anna Freud would call "altruistic surrender" was suppressed during play but emerged in his private life.

> The case of Cyrano de Bergerac. "Cyrano de Bergerac is the tale of a French nobleman who has a big nose and therefore surrenders his love for his beautiful cousin by altruistically supporting a dull-witted rival by providing the rival suitor with passionate words and songs that woe the beautiful cousin" (Rostand, 1897). This is a good example to giving up one's own needs in order to further the needs of a rival. The more modern film "Green Book" starring Viggo Mortensen plays on the same kind of altruistic surrender when the black master pianist provides his simple-minded driver with kind words to woe and comfort the driver's wife while they are far away. Altruistic surrender is often problematic since it leads to little satisfaction.

Case Study #2: The athlete who perpetually perfects their craft in order to display it to fans is a form of altruism. The athlete is like an artist who creates their craft and proudly gives this as a gift to the world (Greenacre, 1957). The athlete who sacrifices all for the pleasure and needs of others describes most professional and elite amateur athletes. One such athlete was discussed in Chapter 18 on the defense of overcompensation. This woman grew up with both primary immune deficiency disorder as well as Ehlers-Danlos syndrome which meant she was not permitted to play sports. In her twenties, she had a car accident where she nearly lost her leg, had multiple surgeries to repair it and was told she would be wheelchair bound. Rather than give up, she embarked upon a career of handcycling and now participates in ultra-endurance races, including the 930-mile "Race Across America" which starts in California, goes over the Rocky Mountains, through the desert and ends in Colorado. Her career is an act of courage given her disability and the amount of pain she endures, and she is now a well-known athlete who is having a documentary made about her life. This is a demonstration of what Vaillant calls the highest-level defense by managing defeat, pain, suffering and adversity through constructive and gratifying service to others. This athlete is acting as the ultimate role model of strength and fortitude. One can easily argue that all professional, Olympic-level and amateur athletes are altruistically serving others by setting an example of what it means to be disciplined, strong and perseverant. The pros are paid for this service and the amateurs receive a sense of gratification and ultimate purpose by developing and displaying their skills. Sports is like most of the performing arts in that it rarely pays off financially but it does offer the athlete an enormous sense of altruistic gratification, purpose, pride and meaning. Sports can be seen as a religious calling, and when the athlete accepts the call, as this athlete did, they enter into the realm where their suffering is transcended through the gift they offer. We never want to pathologize athletes who suffer and give back to the world as exemplars of fortitude, heroism and strength.

Key Points

- Altruism is defined as a high-level defense characterized by dedicated service to others and usually referred to as performing acts of charity.
- Altruistic surrender or masochism was first described by Anna Freud and is seen as dysfunctional and self-defeating.
- More modern views of altruism as those of George Vaillant describe altruism as a high-level and mature defense.
- Extreme sacrificial attitudes in sports can produce self-defeat by being too compassionate or by taking pity on the opponent.

Reflective Questions

- Describe the positive aspects of altruism in sports.
- Now describe the negative aspects of altruistic surrender in sports.
- Do you think that being a team player by passing more than shooting can be a sign of altruism. However, describe the way giving away opportunities to a teammate can be a fear of risk taking.

Exercise Drills for Best Performance

Drill #1: For teams that lack chemistry and camaraderie, it is wise for the coach and each player to provide positive reinforcement to the players. Vocalize your support for teammates by cheering and complimenting at least once per game.

Tips for Best Performance

For teams that lack chemistry and camaraderie, it is wise for the coach to provide positive reinforcement to the players who display a supportive attitude. This is effective for the players on the bench who feel left out and perhaps resentful and jealous of those on the field. Coaches can reinforce and vocally praise players who are cheering on their teammates. This kind of reinforcement helps create an altruistic attitude on the team and can be contagious and very useful.

Recommended Viewing

The film "Rocky," written, starring and directed by Sylvester Stallone, is a film about a down and out bum who, through sacrifice and discipline, became an inspiration to others.

Frankl, V.E. (1959) *Man's Search for Meaning*. Hodder & Stoughton.
Freud, A. (1966) *The Ego and the Mechanisms of Defense*. International University Press.
Greenacre, P. (1957) The Childhood of the Artist. *The Psychoanalytic Study of the Child*, 12: 47–72, 58.
Megna, M. (2024) *Pet Ownership Statistics*. Forbes Advisor, 1–45.
Rostand, E. (1897) *Cyrano de Bergerac*. Dover.
Vaillant, G. (1992) *Ego Mechanisms of Defense*. American Psychiatric Press.
Winnicott, D. (1971) *Playing and Reality*. Routledge.

27 The Anticipation Defense as the Definitive Pre-Game Routine

Anticipation is defined as the realistic planning for future discomfort and emotional reactions (DiGiuseppe & Perry, 2021). When an athlete establishes a pre-game plan to deal with game-time emotions, they are employing their anticipation defense. This defense is aligned with the cognitive/behavioral goal-setting techniques (Meisner, 1985; Weinberg & Butt, 2016). The defense of anticipation allows the athlete to consider realistic alternative responses to any problems that may arise before and during competition. The defense of anticipation relates to "Murphy's Law," which says to expect that whatever can go wrong will go wrong, so make sure you have a plan to deal with it. As with all defense mechanisms, it can be effective but it does have its limits as we will explore in the case study.

The best planning I've ever witnessed was Tiger Woods, as he prepared for the 2002 U.S. Open at Bethpage, the year he won. I had inside the ropes access to the event and stood behind him as he prepared to play his last round on Sunday. He rehearsed each shot he would hit that day, from first to last and discussed with his caddie Steve Williams both the predicted wind direction and then club selection for every shot he would play. After making each decision, he would hit the shot on the range and go on to the next shot, discussing club and wind and rehearsing shot after shot. His anticipation and planning of each shot was remarkable. This strategy of anticipation was undoubtedly learned from his father who was a Green Beret and knew the importance of planning. I wouldn't be surprised if Sun Tzu's "The Art of War" was on Earl Woods bookshelf. "The Art of War" was written in 500 B.C. but remains one of the classic studies of war and how to prepare for any and all contingencies.

The following two cases reveal the effectiveness of the anticipation defense and also its limits.

Case #1: This athlete presented with anxiety, overthinking, lacking in spontaneity and feeling "frozen" during play. He had become ineffective as a forward on his elite-level travel soccer and was in danger of being benched and removed from the starting lineup. The coaches and the parents were all in a hurry to have this player fixed and were results oriented in their approach and expectations regarding therapy. Rather than lose this patient with a premature termination, I embarked on a teaching process where we anticipated his anxious emotions before they emerged and created a strategy of humorous self-talk, banter the locker room and using trash talk while on the field. Given his good intelligence, he was able to learn these techniques in short order and his play improved quickly and dramatically. The strategy of anticipating game-time pressure and forestalling it with positive self-talk and banter worked well and we parted ways after 20 sessions. He seemed happy and his parents and coaches were as well. Approximately, one year later, I received a call from him asking to return to therapy. When he came in, I asked him what we needed to work on and he said:

> Well, Doc, we were successful in dealing with my anxiety on the field but then something else happened. I now have compulsions like having to repeat myself when talking and I have lots of ruminations and doubt as to whether I'm working out enough. I even now have an obsession about my tongue when I am talking.

These are standard symptoms felt with athletes with obsessive compulsive disorder. It appears that his on the field anxiety helped him to contain and express the deeper anxieties held within his unconscious. We were able to suppress and remove his performance anxiety only to have it shatter into a variety of off the court symptoms. This case is a good example of symptom substitution. Without addressing the underlying causes of a player's anxiety, the application of suppressive techniques will inevitably make the athlete vulnerable to other off-the-field symptomology. This case reveals the inherent danger of cognitive/behavioral interventions. Without insight gained through discussion, there can be no resolution of underlying issues. As I have said elsewhere, this is akin to taking aspirin when you are diagnosed with cancer. The pain may be removed but the cancer will spread.

    This case tells us that symptom substitution is a real phenomenon and that the use of even high-level defenses like anticipation must be handled with care and with patience. Embracing quick fixes simply will not remove the danger that lies beneath the surface and within the unconscious. Until these inner demons are faced, understood and worked through, any hasty embrace of suppressive techniques can lead to disaster in other areas of the athlete's life.

The Anticipation Defense as the Definitive Pre-Game Routine

Key Points

- Anticipation is the defense of realistic planning for future discomfort or negative emotional reactions. It is considered a mature and adaptive defense.
- However, the hasty use of pre-planning for future problems without careful consideration of the underlying causes of the anxiety may result in improvement on the field of play but producing problems in other areas of the athlete's life.

Reflective Questions

- What is the meaning of "Murphy's Law"?
- Pick a sport and outline what can go wrong before, during and after a game.
- Now, write out how you will handle each of the problems pinpointed in the above question.

Exercise Drills for Best Performance

- Drill #1: On a piece of paper describe three things that can produce problems before and three things that can go wrong during a game. Now, describe how you are going to handle these events should they occur. As an example, one could say that before a game, one may be held up in traffic. How will you deal with this possibility. During a tennis match, your opponent may try to cheat by making a bad call. How will you handle this?

Tips for Best Performance

It is always wise to assess the many events that could throw you off during any tournament or game. The best example of this is Novak Djokovic during his final match in the 2019 Wimbledon men's singles finals against crowd favorite Roger Federer. Djokovic understood and predicted that he would be greeted with silence or booing every time he won a point against Federer and rehearsed in his mind to experience the booing as cheering. This mental trick was a perfect example of anticipation of a negative event, and his preparation allowed him to win that match. When you are playing competitively, there are many things that can go wrong, including the weather, wind, rain delays, missed shots, someone who cheats, unwanted comments or distractions, bad bounces, bad calls, etc., it is best to have a plan for each event so that he can remain poised and steady and not lose focus or composure.

Further Reading

Tsu, S. (1910) *The Art of War* (trans. L. Giles). Barnes and Noble Classics.

References

Di Giuseppe, M. & Perry, C. (2021) The Hierarchy of Defense Mechanisms: Assessing Defensive Functioning with the Defense Mechanisms Rating Scales Q-Sort. *Frontiers in Psychology*. Vol. 12, Article 718440, 1–23.

Meisner, W. (1985) Theories of Personality and Psychopathology: Classical Psychoanalysis. In *Comprehensive Textbook of Psychiatry/IV* Vol. 1 (Eds. H. Kaplan & B. Sadock). Williams and Wilkins, 337–418.

Weinberg, R. & Butt, J. (2016) Goal-Setting and Sport Performance, Research Findings and Practical Applications. In *Sport and Exercise Psychology, Global Perspectives and Fundamental Concepts* (Eds. A. Papalioannou & D. Hackfort). Routledge, 343–355.

28 Asceticism and the Renunciation of Pleasure in a Long-Distance Cyclist

Asceticism is defined as the elimination of pleasurable pursuits in an effort to achieve pride and efficacy through renunciation (Vaillant, 1992). Asceticism has a long history which predates psychoanalysis by many centuries. The word asceticism derives from the ancient Greek work "to exercise" or "to train"' and the term is generally understood to mean the denial of physical pleasure or desire to attain an ideal or goal. It implies a militaristic Spartan-like and moral lifestyle. Asceticism is the foundation of stoicism, and both Buddhism and Christianity cultivate asceticism with their emphasis on celibacy, fasting and the renunciation of worldly pleasure. A popular example of living an ascetic lifestyle is the book "Walden; Life in the Woods" by Henry David Thoreau written in 1854. Thoreau was a transcendentalist who decided to spend two years living a Spartan-like life in the woods, stripping away all superfluous luxuries and living an austere life. The fact that this book is so well-known suggests a general awareness of the value of this kind of ascetic life.

With regards to sports, it is a commonly held belief that boxers should abstain from sexual pleasure the night before a fight. You may recall that when Tiger Woods married, there was a flurry of articles voicing concern that the comforts and pleasures of marriage would drain his energy and distract him from golf (Willis, 2004). You may not have noticed, but in films, most superhero characters like Superman, Spiderman and Batman go without female companionship, ostensibly to allow them to devote all of their time and energy to saving people.

The modern world is filled with great abundance, yet all this abundance does not seem to produce either happiness or contentment. Asceticism remains a valuable approach to a life of meaning, given the general emptiness felt in consumer culture. Many athletes are excellent examples of the ascetic life, sacrificing ease and pleasure and leading as austere disciplined life in order to attain physical excellence. Psychologically, asceticism implies an embrace of a moral tone with a fully conscious rejection of all base pleasures which enables the athlete to obtain gratification and a sense of pride from their militaristic discipline. Jockeys are forced into this kind of asceticism regarding food as well. When Jose Santos was the world's winningest jockey, he would often take the red eye and fly from California to New York for a big race. On this flight, he would allow himself to eat only four peanuts cut into quarters as his only meal during the six-hour flight.

Tiger Woods' practice of asceticism: The ascetic attitude of golfing superstar Tiger Woods was demonstrated in his extreme work ethic and his dietary habits. His Spartan-like attitude toward fitness transformed his body into that of an NFL linebacker, and by so doing, he transformed professional golf into a sport played by strong fit athletes who worked out every day. As an example of Woods' work ethic, Woods was leading the 2002 British Open after three rounds, and on Saturday night, before the last round while his competitors were inside the clubhouse drinking and relaxing, he was seen on the range at 9 PM still hitting shots. And when Woods won an event, he would celebrate by allowing himself to indulge in eating McDonald hamburgers for one day. And immediately following this, he went back to his strict diet. His asceticism was derived from the combination of his mother's Buddhist upbringing and his father's training as a Green Beret.

It usually takes a fanatic focus on an ascetic lifestyle to get to the top of one's sport. However, such single-minded focus can have detrimental effects on the body, the mind, the emotions and one's social life (Beckman, 2023). The choice of asceticism in athletes often excludes adequate rest and recovery and inevitably leads to burnout, flat performance, increased illnesses and injury. Often, the work one engages in with professional athletes is to encourage them to overcome their workaholic like asceticism.

This chapter will discuss the choice of a rigid ascetic life in two athletes I have worked with. Their extraordinary drive and austere lifestyle led to success on the playing field, but it also produced problems as well.

<u>Case study of professional wrestler:</u> This MMA wrestler was seen by me for over three years. About halfway through our work together, I could see that his incessant traveling, fitness work and competitive schedule was earning him good money but taking a toll on his body, leading to exhaustion. He had just returned home from an event in California and was not feeling well at the time and needed a rest. He was suddenly invited to compete in a major event in South America. I advised him against this but given the money and prestige involved, he decided to go. He competed well enough in the event but

upon return contracted pneumonia which led to COVID and a hospital stay of two weeks. He nearly died in the hospital, and it took him over six months to fully recover. This only occurred because his sacrificial, overworked and ascetic lifestyle compromised his immune system to a dangerous degree.

Case study of a long-distance runner: This patient came to my office for direction and support in areas of work and family, and although he was not a competitive athlete, we frequently discussed his exercise and sports life. He was an Iron Man contestant who would rise at 5 AM every day to either run, cycle and swim for three hours prior to work. He led a disciplined, non-complaining and militaristic lifestyle. He would often speak about his efforts and I often wondered if all of this energy and suffering was worth it. He already had back pain, knee pain and knee surgery. I was in awe of this athlete's ability to resist pain and remain disciplined whether it was hot or cold, raining or sunny, whether he was tired or rested. Over time, we began to explore his motives for competing in Iron Man events. His disciplined lifestyle began after high school. As a youngster, he was overweight and was ridiculed for this weight problem both in school and at home and was nicknamed "Tubby." His mother was unavailable and his father was a cold and disciplined Marine. In order to cope with the lack of love, the strictness with which he was raised, and the bullying due to his weight, he decided to adopt an austere, militaristic ascetic lifestyle which served to repress and suppress all of the negative effects within. The result was that he looked healthy and trim which garnered him some praise but not nearly enough to compensate for all the pain he had to endure.

Over time, we came to realize that his intense exercise regimen and his dietary restrictions served to defend him for the painful effects of his childhood. As time went on, he slowly relinquished his severe lifestyle, began to sleep in more, eat a normal diet and began to feel better in mood. This case signifies the way that a mature defense like asceticism can be both adaptive, shown by his fitness but also maladaptive in that his asceticism produced injuries, exhaustion and irritability.

> Buddhism and the Middle Way: One of the most common tenets in Buddhism is referred to as the Middle Way. When Buddha awakened into enlightenment, he began to teach the Middle Way which means that one should neither indulge in extreme sensual pleasures nor self-mortification or extremes of asceticism. Although this sounds like a simple rule to follow, but in fact, it's extremely difficult to achieve. Psychologically, it is a sign that the person has achieved true mental health and has the ability to lead a balanced life.

Key Points

- Asceticism is a defense defined as the elimination of pleasurable pursuits in an effort to achieve pride and a sense of efficacy through the power of renunciation.
- Asceticism derives from the Greek "to train" or "to exercise."
- Asceticism has been seen for centuries and used by Sophists, Stoics, Buddhists and Christians.
- This defense is a favorite of high-level professional athletes, with Tiger Woods as a good example.
- Despite the fact that asceticism is considered a mature defense, when practiced in excess, it leads to burnout, injuries and illness.

Reflective Questions

- How would you define asceticism?
- Describe one ascetic practice in your life. This may derive form a religious practice or from a sporting experience.
- Why must athletes practice an ascetic lifestyle if they expect to win?

Exercise Drills for Best Performance

- Drill #1: Asceticism or the renunciation of pleasure is a good trait, but in order to maintain it, one must feel it has a clear purpose and one must engage it in a way that is tolerable so that you can maintain it as a lifestyle. A useful and surprisingly difficult ascetic practice is to get to bed early enough to insure eight hours sleep. If one must rise at 6 AM, this means you need to be sleeping by 10 PM. This in turn means you must be willing to give up television and social media by 9:30 and go to bed. To commit to this, one must understand the value of eight hours of sleep. Adequate sleep has great value since it allows your immune system to function well and this prevents illness.

Tips for Best Performance

Asceticism or the renunciation of easy pleasures is a good trait, and in order to maintain it, one must also take pride in yourself for your discipline and reward yourself with weekly pleasures. Mother Theresa was a true ascetic, but when she was staying overnight in a hotel after giving a speech, she would treat herself to a treat of a single chocolate wafer that the hotel leaves on the pillow.

Further Reading

Walden; or, Life in the Woods by Henry David Thoreau.

References

Beckman, J. (2023) Meaning and Meaninglessness in Elite Sport. In *Routledge Handbook of Mental Health in Elite Sport* (Eds. I. Nixdorf, R. Nixdorf, J. Beckman, S. Martin, & T. MacIntyre). Routledge, 31–44.

Vaillant, G. (1992) *Ego Mechanisms of Defense*. American Psychiatric Press.

Willis, G. (June 16, 2004) *For Better, Not Worse*. In New York Post.

29 How Athletes Use Humor to Cope with Stress

The defense of humor is defined as the expression of feelings without bringing undo discomfort to the self or to others (Vaillant, 1992.). This valuable trait reveals intelligence and the ability to rise above pain. Presidents John Kennedy and Ronald Reagan both mastered the art of humor which they used to charm the press and rise above many potential controversies. Every successful businessperson I have treated has possessed a fully functioning and well-defined sense of humor. I call this trait the "likability factor." Some of our most beloved athletes have used humor well. Mohammed "I am the Greatest!" Ali was renowned for his sense of humor and golfing great Lee Trevino was nicknamed "Merry Mex" based upon his wit. In the world of tennis, we have Novak "The Jokester" Djokovic who uses jokes and mimicry to entertain the crowd.

One of Sigmund Freud's most important books was "Jokes and Their Relation to the Unconscious," a text he returned to and revised six times. Freud considered humor as one of man's most adaptive defenses (Freud, 1905). My dissertation was on the use of humor and I recall asking Leonard Krasner who was chair of the Clinical Division what he thought of the subject of humor as a research area, and he said "The ability to joke and use humor is a measure of high intelligence and it ought to be used as a subtest on IQ tests."

The use of humor is evidence that the athlete can look directly at what is painful by expressing the pain with wit, jokes and a smile. Mark Nesti of the English Premier League is, to my knowledge, the only sport psychologist to write about the use of humor and banter in the locker room, a method athletes use to of relax and ease team tension (Nesti, 2000). In this chapter, we will explore how the establishment of a sense of joking and humor can be used in the locker room, on the court and in therapy to help produce a more relaxed state of mind in an athlete.

> Canadian humor: It is noteworthy that Canada has produced an abundance of comic geniuses, including Jim Carrey, Mike Myers, Martin Short and Dan Aykroyd. All of these comedians have an interesting combination of humility and wittiness. Their humor is non-threatening or what Freud called non-tendentious or playful, harmless humor (Freud, 1905). I would say that the Canadian personality makes good use of the defense of humor.

<u>Case #1:</u> This is the case of a talented high school hockey player in a private school who was on scholarship but was plagued by regressed feelings of depersonalization or what he described as "being out of sync." I asked him what he thought would help with this feeling of being disconnected with the flow of the game, and he said "maybe if I joked around more." This patient was a bright athlete, and he was able to employ humor with ease. It also helped that his older sibling was a standup comic which meant that throughout childhood, my patient was constantly being exposed to joking. I encouraged him to start to joke around more, and within a fairly short period of time, he was telling me that his joking in the locker room and on the ice was helping him quite a bit. He would banter and joke in the locker room and play around with trash talk on the ice, and these maneuvers helped him to remain relaxed and get into sync with the flow of the game. His scoring improved as did his mood.

Humor was also of great value in our sessions as well. At the beginning of our work, he was very standoffish, guarded and quiet. Over time, I learned to rely on joking and humor in order to establish trust and a working alliance with him. He relaxed with this technique and slowly opened up to me about a variety of concerns which we have continued to work on.

The critical point of this chapter is to show how an athlete can come in with a regressed, primitive type defense such as depersonalization (see Chapter 7), but how humor can help the athlete to relax both in therapy and on the playing field in such a way that their performance improves and their defensive strategies mature as well.

Key Points

- Humor is a valued trait in virtually all walks of life, including politics, business and sports.
- Freud considered humor to be a highly adaptive mature defense which allowed one to ventilate emotions without discomfort to self or others.

- Joking can be used in the locker room and on the court to help the athlete to express or ventilate feelings and to relax.
- Humor, joking and a lighter touch can help establish a working alliance with athletes who are guarded, standoffish or quiet.

Reflective Questions

- Define humor.
- The comedians Adam Sandler and Jim Carey are two of the most highly paid film stars. Why do you think that is?
- Do you think it's a good idea to be able to joke around and be happy as you play?

Exercise Drills for Best Performance

- Tension, anxiety and anger are part of all competitive sports, and the athlete needs to have coping strategies to handle these emotions. Humor is a very effective method which can be used to ventilate anxiety or anger in such a way that it produces laughter and relaxation. The next time you're under pressure in a game, use some humor and observe its impact on your mood and sense of power. Humor may be the best way to transcend your anxiety and rise above it.

Tips for Best Performance

Tension, anxiety and anger are part of all competitive sports, and the athlete needs to have coping strategies to handle these emotions. Humor is a very effective method which can be used to ventilate anxiety or anger in such a way that it produces laughter and relaxation. If you are an athlete who struggles with anxiety, try joking around as a way of you expressing. This may be the best way to transcend your anxiety.

Further Reading

Sigmund Freud's "Wit and its Relation to the Unconscious."

References

Nesti, M. (2000) *The Psychology of Football*. Routledge.
Freud, S. (1905, 1960) *Jokes and Their Relation to the Unconscious* (trans. into English by J. Strachey & F. Deuticke). Hogarth.
Vaillant, G. (1992) *Ego Mechanisms of Defense, A Guide for Clinicians and Researchers*. American Psychiatric Press.

30 Suppression Used to Manage Competitive Anxiety

Suppression is defined as the mechanism in which the athlete consciously and intentionally avoids thinking about an uncomfortable problem or upcoming event (Vaillant, 1992). Every athlete needs to suppress worries, fears and fantasies as they make their way to the finish line, but many are unable to do so. This ability is commonly referred to as "staying in the moment" and invariably you will hear athletes talk about how they won by saying they "just stayed present" and didn't get ahead of themselves. The moment the athlete begins to fantasize about victory is the moment they lose focus, lose power and lose the game. I believe the ability to suppress the urge to worry or to fantasize separates the winner from the loser.

The behavior modification technique called thought stopping is one way of establishing suppression by asking the patient to close their eyes and visualize the negative thoughts or fantasies and then clapping loudly in their ears to shock them out of this thought. Perhaps because it was so closely aligned with punishment and aversive conditioning, this technique grew out of favor (Wenzlaff & Wegner, 2000).

Case study of suppression: This is the case of an amateur golfer I worked with for three years who also happened to be a world-famous politician. He had a strong desire to improve his golf game and we worked diligently on this. He started as an 18 handicap, and eventually, he played to an 11 handicap after three years of work. But his ability to suppress outside problems was shown in his political life. About one year into our work together, he was accused of having an affair with one of his interns, a scandal that could easily have destroyed his career. Despite months of unrelenting and mostly negative press coverage and the need to hire expensive attorneys to defend himself against these accusations, he remained unfazed and managed to suppress all of this turmoil. He remained in office and did not miss a day's work. I asked him how he managed to deal with this level of stress, and he told me, he was able to compartmentalize the matter. He successfully suppressed all feelings about it and went on to win re-election. This is an extreme example of the power to suppress and compartmentalize thoughts. This politician had a history of violent abuse in childhood, and as McWilliams has stated, there is a strong ability to use suppression and the ability to compartmentalize thoughts in cases of post-traumatic stress disorder (McWilliams, 1994).

> Suppression in an Asian golfer: Years ago, I was working with a 15-year-old Japanese golfer at the New York State Open. As we talked on the putting green, he complained to me that his back was bothering him a great deal. I knew that there were a team of chiropractors in attendance at this event, and I went to the player's father and told him that his son's back was hurting him and that I recommended he get some work done by a chiropractor before teeing off. The father said "No, he doesn't have a back problem." I said that in fact the son did have back problems and was complaining about it, and the father reiterated more strongly "No, my son does not have a back problem." This is a good example of how a cultural norm of pain suppression and pain denial can be transmitted through each generation. The son was being told to deny the pain and so would eventually have to develop a suppressive attitude toward it.

Suppression is a valuable defense for the athlete since it fosters focus and the crucial ability to stay in the moment. However, it should be noted that in extreme cases of trauma or abuse, the suppressive attitude becomes too rigid which can lead to an inflexible thinking style and a lack of creativity.

Key Points
- Suppression is the ability to temporarily avoid thoughts or feelings concerning events in the immediate past or future, and this ability can help the athlete to stay in the moment.
- Thought stopping is one way to teach the ability to suppress thoughts or feelings in order to get the athlete to stay in the moment.
- Compartmentalization is a primitive form of suppression and is based upon dissociation and trauma history.
- Asian golfers are seen as having the ability to suppress fantasy and stay in the moment.

Reflective Questions
- What is the best way to "stay in the moment?"
- How do thoughts about the future or ruminating about the past prevent the athlete from staying in the present?
- How can the technique of "thought stopping" help the athlete to temporarily suppress thoughts of the future?

Exercise Drills for Best Performance

LEARNING HOW TO STAY IN THE MOMENT:

- Drill #1: By teaching your eyes to focus on a spot on the wall as you balance on one leg is a subtle way of staying present and not worrying about falling over. This visual awareness drill is used by golfers to be "target aware." Focusing on a spot on the wall is also effective if you have a fear of needles when in the doctor's office. Train yourself to look at a spot on the wall as the doctor is injecting you rather than looking at the needle going in.
- Drill #2: Thought stopping is good to stay poised and calm on the days leading up to a tournament. When you catch yourself ruminating about the game, say "Stop That," take a deep breath and get busy with something else. This is a good distraction technique that can be used over and over to suppress apprehension and worry.

Tip for Best Performance

LEARNING HOW TO STAY IN THE MOMENT: A drill that teaches you how to stay present is what I call the clock drill. Train yourself to look at your clock only once in the morning, then go about your morning preparation of showering, eating and driving to your job. You will be training your mind to stay focused on what you are doing, and this will prevent you from engaging in distracting behaviors or thoughts. This drill of staying in the moment introduces you to the ability to suppress fantasy or worry. For golfers, this translates into being mentally disciplined during tournament play by not looking at scoreboard and not letting any disruptive experiences or fantasies or worries distract you from the task at hand. Whenever an urge arises which gets them to get ahead of themselves and think of the end result, I train them to say "No, not now, just get back to the task at hand."

References

McWilliams, N. (1994) *Psychoanalytic Diagnosis: Understanding Personality Structure in the Clinical Process*. Guilford Press.

Vaillant, G. (1992) *Ego Mechanisms of Defense, A Guide for Clinicians and Researchers*. American Psychiatric Press.

Wenzlaff, R. & Wegner, D. (2000) Thought Suppression. *Annual Review of Psychology*, 51: 59–91.

31 Sublimation, Aggression and Winning

Sublimation is defined as the channeling of aggressive or sexual instincts into socially sanctioned activities
(McWilliams, 1994). Sport is culture's primary way to channel aggressive drives and is superior to war as a way to express aggression. As a good example, the Olympics is a better way to show national superiority than going to war. Sublimation of aggression provides both pleasure and excitement for the athlete and the fan and is considered to be the most mature defense. In sublimation, our aggressive instincts are acknowledged rather than dammed up as with all of the other defenses. Freud was the first to define sublimation, and he considered it to be a characteristic of a healthy human. Freud also suggested that sublimation was crucial to mental health (Freud, 1961). It may be that one reason people become depressed in the winter (seasonal affective disorder) is that they lose access to their sporting activities due to the cold and the day's early darkness.

George Vaillant considered sublimation to be a high form of defense which allowed for the indirect expression of instincts without marked loss of pleasure (1992). Johan Huizinga, the Dutch cultural historian, suggested that sublimation through the playing of games has significant cultural value by providing bonding, freedom, pride and rules of fair play. He felt that the value of game playing guarantees that sports will remain one of mankind's most healthy habits (Huizinga, 1950).

Mihaly Csikszentmihalyi's popular concept of "flow" is a direct descendant of Freud's concept of sublimation, defining flow as that sublime experience we sometimes obtain filled with joy, creativity and gratification Csikszentmihalyi, 1990). Part of the joy of flow derives from aggressive and sexual instincts that have been tapped into, not repressed but instead channeled appropriately.

Finally, Lenore Terr's book about play (Terr, 1999) addresses the importance of play in adult life, and though she does not rely on the concept of sublimation, she does suggest that sports are crucial to a healthy adult lifestyle.

In this chapter, I will present two cases of sublimation. Each will show how aggression can be successfully channeled or sublimated into a successful sport career.

Case #1: This patient was a golfer who was nationally ranked long-drive contest winner. I recall playing with him in one round where he regularly drove the ball over 350 yards. On the first hole of the round, a short par four of about 320 yards, he drove the green with a 2 iron. On the eleventh hole, a par four of about 420 yards, his drive ended up about 40 yards short of the green. When I asked him what his swing key was as he was about to drive, he said to me "I think of the ball as my swing coaches head and I swing away." This unnerving comment warrants some analysis. His history revealed that he was trained by a fanatic and militaristic swing coach throughout childhood. He was subjected to extreme abuse by this coach who was intimidating and aggressive. He was never able to express any resentment toward the coach and repressed all of his much anger and aggression. However, he was able to vent this aggression by channeling it into his golf swing which produced a very successful and lucrative career as a long-drive champion.

Case #2: Boxing is a physically violent sport with broken noses, shattered eardrums and deep gashes handed out nearly every fight. So, when a boxer walks into my office, I know I am in the presence of someone who is holding in all sorts of aggression. When I first met this fighter, he wanted to learn how to improve his already well-honed killer instinct. During intake, I learned that he had an extremely conflicted relationship with his wife who was domineering, disapproving and at times physically violent toward him. Our work lasted only ten sessions and it largely consisted of using hypnosis to remove any guilt he held regarding hurting his opponents. This simple technique worked remarkably well and he went on to win a number of big fights in the first round. Such is the power of aggression when it gets unleashed. He was now able to freely express his previously repressed and overly controlled aggression. Our work enabled him to replace his defense of repression into the more adaptive defense of sublimation. Years passed by and he would occasionally call me on the phone to say hello and to stay in touch. Addendum: About 15 years after our work together, I called him up to do a piece about him for a newspaper I was writing for. During that interview, I asked him what he recalled about our work together and what was most helpful to him. Without hesitating, he said "Without a doubt what I remember most was that I discovered how much anger I had for my wife. That was the most helpful thing that we did." This surprised me since I was expecting him to recall the hypnosis we did together to remove his repressive barriers. This was a good reminder to me of the power of insight over action. He felt that the gains we made in our work together did not stem from hypnosis but from insight.

Key Points

- Sublimation is defined as the ability to channel your aggressive drives into socially sanctioned activities such as sports.
- Sports and the ability to play games and have fun is crucial to mental health and why sports is so valued in all cultures.
- Sublimation is considered a mature and highly adaptive defense which allows you to feel gratified and satisfied.

Reflective Questions

- Define sublimation and give one example.
- Why is it necessary to sublimate one's aggressive impulses?
- The reason there are an abundance of rules in sports is because sports requires the athlete to tap into aggression. Explain what is meant by this statement.

Tips for Best Performance

Many athletes inhibit aggression out of unconscious guilt or anxiety that it is unsportsmanlike to be too aggressive or too cocky. They resort to using repression or reaction formation which serves to inhibit their ability to win. Try to recognize that aggression and even anger can be useful fuel by providing you with the energy and power you need to win. Look carefully at your history to see if you have been repressing your aggression out of a childhood fear of retaliation from a father or big brother. This kind of insight can help you to shift your aggressive stance on the field. Find a good aggressive role model to emulate. Insight and role modeling an alpha athlete can be helpful.

Further Reading

Huizinga, J. (1950) *Homo Ludens, A Study of the Play Element in Culture*. The Beacon Press.

References

Csikszentmihalyi, M. (1990) *Flow: The Psychology of Optimal Experience*. Harper Perennial Modern Classics.

Freud, S. (1961) *Civilization and Its Discontents* (trans. J. Strachey). Norton and Company.

Huizinga, J. (1950) *Homo Ludens, A Study of the Play Element in Culture*. The Beacon Press.
McWilliams, N. (1994) *Psychoanalytic Diagnosis: Understanding Personality Structure in the Clinical Process*. The Guildford Press.
Terr, L. (1999) *Beyond Love and Work, Why Adults need to Play*. Scribner.
Vaillant, G. (1992) *Ego Mechanisms of Defense: A Guide for Clinicians and Researchers*. American Psychiatric Press.

32 Sublimation of the Sexual Impulse in Sports

Sexual sublimation is defined as the gratification of a sexual impulse but whose aim is changed from a socially objectionable one to a more socially valued one. Sublimation is the ability to channel sexual or aggressive impulses without damming them up. There are many examples of the way sexuality is channeled through sports.

There is almost nothing written about the way sexuality is sublimated in sports because the entire edifice of civilization itself is predicated upon the denial of the power of sexuality. Freud once wrote:

> society does not wish to be reminded of this precarious portion of its foundation. It has no interest in the recognition of the strength of sexual instincts or in the demonstration of the importance of sexual life to the individual. On the contrary, with an educational aim in view, it has set about diverting attention from that whole field of ideas.
>
> (Freud, 1917)

I frequently hear athletes tell me they want to lose weight in order to look more attractive to fans, and I continuously tell them their business requires strength and food intake and not good looks.

Proof of the use of and concern with sexuality during competitive play is seen every day. Physically, the athlete's heart races, the pupils dilate and they sweat, all physiological states similar to the way the body reacts during sexual intercourse. Michael Commons of Harvard College gave a talk where he discussed openly the sexual appeal of athletes who are all so fit, healthy and good looking and thus become the object of desire for many adoring fans (America at Play Conference, 1996).

Symbolically, there are numerous examples of the way sports mimics sexual intercourse. When the winner is crowned in NASCAR events, a huge champagne bottle is handed to the winning driver who is expected to de-cork it, shake it and squirt the foaming liquid all over the crowd.

This same ritual is performed at the end of every Ryder Cup match in golf. The similarity between this ritual and the penis having an orgasm is undeniable.

Concerning uniforms, the attire worn by beach volley-ballers is much less covered up than with other sports, as it considers the warmer climate and how the sand can interfere with the athlete's movements and comfort. Although this uniform is worn for practical reasons, it can be argued that some fans are likely to enjoy watching the sport more because of the uniform's more revealing nature.

Suarez-Orozco studied the popular songs that Argentine fans chant during soccer games (1999). He discovered that most of the chants being sung refer to the hometown team being made up of men, the visiting team consisting of girls and that each time the hometown team's ball penetrated the net of the visiting team, it symbolized that they were men and that the visiting team was converted into girls.

One professional soccer player I know told me her college coach would encourage his female players to lose weight. This coach was eventually brought up on charges of sexual abuse by two of his players.

The obvious point here is that, just as Freud suggested, sexuality is an ever-present and compelling fact of life and plays a large role in athletes' lives on and off the field. The following three cases demonstrate the way sexuality insinuates itself into the world of sports and why it must be addressed in order to help the athlete to manage it.

Case Study #1: This teenage figure skater was brought to my office by her father who was concerned that she was not performing up to potential. At the time, this player was 13 but well-developed. Good looks are generally considered to be of benefit, but when you're a young girl, skating in front of large crowds, it is virtually impossible to manage that psychologically. Advanced secondary sexual characteristics for girls is usually problematic and often causes anxiety and self-consciousness (Kugler et al., 2017). In this case, this young figure skater became anxious and self-conscious as she performed. We discovered the roots of her anxiety by talking frankly about this with both her and her parents. This alleviated her self-consciousness to some degree.

Case Study #2: I met this female tennis player at a conference I was speaking at. She was a club champion at her tennis club and wanted help in managing her anxiety as she played. As we worked, she began to describe how much shame, dread and anxiety she felt while playing in front of big crowds. As she freely associated with why this dread was so deep, she shared that as a child, she was unusually adorable, and she was repeatedly asked to dance and perform in front of her parents' friends on a Saturday night. It seems that the narcissistic gratification was so great that she experienced it as a shameful act. Gabbard (1997) has written that the roots of stage fright are often based upon shame. It appears that her physical beauty, coupled with her physical talent placed her in front of crowds and that this was too much attention which was in turn causing this anxiety, dread and shame in her. Over time, we discussed the connection between her present anxiety of playing in front of crowds and her past shame. She believed that the crowds who watched her play tennis somehow knew about her past shame. Insight into this connection helped free her of some of her performance anxiety.

Case Study #3: This 50-year-old amateur golfer came to my office during his quest to qualify for the Champions Tour, the professional golf tour for men of over 50 years of age. He was a bright golfer but was overwhelmed by negative thinking as he played. We used a number of techniques to help him to overcome his anxiety and negative thinking but nothing had much of an impact. However, one day, he came in the office smiling and said he had finally found a technique that worked to quell his anxiety, fears and negative thinking on the course. When I asked him what he did, he said that the tips came from his wife. She advised him to fall in love with each hole rather than fight it as an enemy. She suggested that when he looked at the hole from the tee to find the beauty of it and to feel positive. Granted, this is not a direct use of sexuality to enhance performance, but it is closely aligned to sex in that she said to introduce the feelings of love and beauty into his approach to his game, and in this case, it proved effective.

Key Points

- Sexual sublimation is defined as the channeling of sexual instincts and urges into a socially sanctioned activity.
- There is ample evidence that sexuality is a part of sports.
- Symbolically, one observes illusions to sexual orgasm when NASCAR or Formula I car drivers shake the big champagne bottle and squirt the cheering crowd with foam.
- Freud suggested that sex was a prime mover in most human activity but that most are in deep denial about this fact.
- I reviewed two cases of female athletes who were the subject of inappropriate attention and admiration which in turn caused anxiety and self-consciousness and hindered their performances.

Reflective Questions

- Give an example to sexuality in sports. You could use examples from beach volleyball, figure skating, diving or swimming.

- How do you think sexuality is channeled by the athlete?
- Why do you think NASCAR drivers shake up the champagne bottle and squirt it on the crowd?

Exercise Drills for Best Performance

One could argue that athletes have an urge to look their best, whilst competing in their sports, especially when being viewed by large crowds, or if the event is being televised. This often leads athletes to diet in excess in order to look better. This is almost always ill-advised. Far more important than being sexually attractive as you play, the athlete needs to be well nourished with food.

Tips for Best Performance

Playing in front of crowds can be daunting, and can lead to feelings of self-consciousness, anxiety and embarrassment. These impulsive feelings, as well as general stage fright, can be difficult to overcome when you are expected to play in front of groups of people on a regular basis. To help ease these worries, you could benefit from exposing yourself more gradually to larger crowds. This could be deciding to not practice alone and instead in front of close family and friends. Or joining a club that will put you in contact with more players who play at a similar level to you, and will help you build up confidence. Alternatively, if you do find your performance is being hindered, you may think about joining a club or gym with the desire to become healthier, whether that be building muscle, developing stamina or losing weight. It is essential to remember that the people who are attending matches are there as they enjoy the sport and want to see you play well. If there is external stress that is impacting your play, consider what is it that is worrying me? Is it something mental or physical? And what measures can I take to lessen the stress I put on myself?

Recommended Viewing

An interesting take on the role of sexual desire in athletes can be seen in Luca Guadagnino's 2024 film *Challengers*, starring Zendaya, Mike Faist and Josh O'Connor. Focusing on the role of hyper-sexuality in sport, it offers a unique perspective into the role of lust, desire and adrenaline in tennis. This fictional story looks at how physical attraction and sexual impulses can surface both on and off the court.

References

Common, M. (1996) *America at Play Conference, Long Island Institute of Psychoanalysis*. Nassau County Medical Center.

Freud, S. (1917) *Introductory Lectures on Psycho-Analysis, The Standard Edition of the Complete Psychological Works of Sigmund Freud* (Ed. Strachey). W.W. Norton and Company, 3124–3501.

Gabbard, G. (1997) The Vicissitudes of Shame in Stage Fright. In *Work and Its Inhibitions* (Eds. C. Socarides & S. Kramer). International Universities Press. 209–220.

Kugler, K., Vasilenko, S., Butera, N., & Coffman, D. (2017) Long-Term Consequences of Early Sexual Initiation on Young Adult Health; A Causal Inference. *Journal of Early Adolescence*, 37(5): 662–676.

Suarez-Orozco, M. (1999) A Psychoanalytic Study of Argentine Soccer. In *Psychoanalysis and Culture at the Millennium*. Eds. Ginsburg, N. & Ginsburg, R. Yale University, 64–95.

Part 4
Odds and Ends

33 The Weakening of Defense Mechanisms with Age

The increasing proneness to yipping and other forms of anxiety in the older athlete is well-known and suggests that their defense mechanisms weaken with age. They are less able to manage competitive stress as they once did. If we search the literature of developmental changes in the ability to handle competitive anxiety in the older athlete, we come up empty. There is virtually nothing written about how the athletes' defenses decay or weaken with age. Sigmund Freud, Melanie Klein and Donald Fairbairn had little to say about defensive changes occurring with age and even psychoanalytic research scholars such as George Vaillant failed to discuss defensive shifts brought on by aging. Vaillant's suggested that old age was a time for the mature person to preserve the collective products of mankind by employing the defense of altruism to enhance one's life (Vaillant, 1977). Victor Frankl's logotherapy (1959) and M. Agronin's work with the elderly (2010) both suggest that the older person seek and find meaning in life as their instinctual energies decline, but little effort is made in how to do so.

Freud's position regarding the treatment of older patients was pessimistic at best when he wrote "near or above the age of fifty, the elasticity of the mental processes, on which treatment depends, is as a rule lacking-old people are no longer educable." (1905, p. 264). As the saying goes 'you can't teach an old dog new tricks'.

It is likely that the older athlete's defensive collapse is due to the accumulation of traumatic failures that can no longer be repressed and they become less able to cope with anxiety. Let us explore in depth a typical case of an aging athlete who feels increased anxiety during competition.

This professional tennis player consulted with me at the age of 62. In his youth, he was able to win events; if not win, he would place highly in tournaments, bring home sizable checks and rarely if ever feel much anxiety. As a child, he grew up deprived, in poverty, without a father and whose mother was alcoholic and psychotic. He witnessed many of her psychotic episodes, including talking to people not present, walking in the streets naked and

DOI: 10.4324/9781003436270-38

throwing large amounts of money out the window. Despite these traumatic events, he was able to repress it and go on to a successful professional tennis career up until the age of about 60. At this point, he played on the senior tour and he began to perform less effectively and found himself feeling more anxiety, and when he was in the finals, he would begin to overthink and have self-doubt. Instead of feeling confident and focused as he once did just a few years ago, he now found himself overtrying and failing more than winning. He was no longer able to suppress his anxiety, and he had regressed into intellectualization, a less mature defense. His accumulated stress over the years was now breaking through. In addition, as we age, we have less energy to serve our suppressive needs and regress into intellectualization. Agronin (2010) has suggested that the energy it takes to repress early childhood dynamics and therefore those self-defeating dynamics reemerge.

It is clear that aging athletes tend to regress in function, lose confidence and experience more anxiety as they age. One will hear the argument that this is inevitable given that aging brings decay on a physical level. But it is also clear to me that physical deterioration does not account for the whole story. It is likely that with less physical energy, the athlete will be faced with the emergence of both recent and early childhood losses that have not been resolved and thus seek expression. Needless to say this remains an uncharted territory in the field of sport psychology and again calls for a series of good dissertations in the field of the defenses used in aging athlete.

What I did in this case was to explore and discuss both recent unresolved losses and then childhood dynamics so that he would not need to utilize so much energy on repressing these feelings.

Key Points

- It is evident that athletes are prone to feeling more anxiety as they age.
- One reason for increases in the experience of anxiety as athletes age is because their defenses become weaker.
- Defense mechanisms require athletes to use up energy, and as the athlete ages, he or she has less energy to do so.

Reflective Questions

- Give an example of an older athlete who refused to retire and what were the consequences.
- Why do athletes deny aging? Does it have something to do with losing the spotlight?
- How would you help an aging athlete who is angry because he has lost his power?

Exercise Drills for Best Performance

- Drill #1: If you are getting older and see that your performance is declining and you are feeling more anxious and less able to handle pressure, there is much you can do about this. The essential issue is to face up to the fact that with age comes fatigue. The best thing to do is to sit with a therapist and articulate your predicament. The ability to verbalize your loss of skill set will free you to relax and also allow you to begin to explore other less physical forms of sublimation.
- Drill #2: Design an ethically appropriate framework for how a coach could support an athlete who is struggling with the idea of growing old, or who has recently undergone a major surgery that has impacted their sporting abilities.

Tips for Best Performance

If you are getting older and feel more anxiety, it is wise to do two things. First you need to re-acquaint yourself or learn how to suppress anxiety (see Chapter 32). Then, you need to discuss and resolve recent losses as well as early childhood dynamics so that you need not expend so much energy in repressing them.

Recommended Reading

George Vaillant's Adaptation "To Life."
Agronin, M. (2010) *Therapy with Older Clients: Key Strategies for Success*. W. W. Norton.
Frankl, V. (1959) *Man's Search for Meaning*. Beacon Press.
Freud, S. (1905, 1964) On Psychotherapy. In *The Standard Edition of the Complete Works of Sigmund Freud* (Ed. & trans. J. Strachey). Hogarth, 255–268.
Vaillant, G. (1977) *Adaptation to Life*. Harvard University Press.

34 Meditation and Prayer as a Way to Find the Zone

One of the primary goals for an athlete is to find the zone, a place of detachment, peace and focus. One of the primary goals of a Buddhist monk is to find nirvana, a place of detachment, peace and focus. Both the zone and nirvana require an uncluttered mind. Let us explore the possible benefits of meditation for the anxious overthinking athlete. It is reasonable to suggest that there are more athletes using some form of prayer to cope with competitive anxiety than positive self-talk, psychological insight or any other sport psychology tool. Buddhism was established 2,600 years ago and its emphasis on detachment and meditation may offer some benefit for athletes seeking focus and peace.

It is clear that psychoanalysis and religion represent opposing paradigms with psychoanalysis encouraging an exploration of the unconscious through free association whereas religion emphasizing the use of prayer or meditation to suppress thought. Buddhism entails a commitment to meditation which fosters detachment. Could Buddhist detachment through meditation help an athlete detach from the noise of competition and enter the zone? Every athlete desires this state but very few are able to get there at will. With the exception of Csikszentmihalyi (1990), no persuasive theory exists which provides much insight into these matters. Fatigue, distractions, anxiety, anger, stress, worry, pressure, fans, money and injury all block entrance to the zone. The competitive sports environment is designed to rob one's peace of mind so the ability to withdraw into oneself is a crucial ability (Kaminoff & Proshansky, 1982).

Buddhism preaches detachment through renunciation of desire, expectations and thought (Gorkum, 1996). Buddhist monks live a monastic ascetic life cloistered away from the temptations of ordinary life. The goal of much work with athletes is to help them find that cloistered state of mind where they ignore distractions from the crowds, the parents, the coaches and the media. Athletes perform best if they are focused on the task at hand and not wasting energy socially, physically or mentally. Professional teams will attempt to get the athletes into a state of detachment on game day by getting the team to the stadium hours before game time and structure their morning with meetings, physical therapy, food intake and pep talks. Olympics athletes are detached from regular life by being cloistered in the Olympic training camp for weeks and months at a time. All this isolation is designed to help the athlete detach from real life and enter the zone.

The Buddhist concept of detachment has a similar goal to that of the athlete in training. The monk is expected to fully separate and individuate into a state of nirvana or enlightenment. Buddhist monks spend their entire life in an effort to gain enlightenment. They live cloistered lives, detached from the world and meditate regularly. This requires discipline, and meditation takes time, but the rewards are great. An enlightened monk who meditates well is said to have the ability to levitate. I'm not sure of that but I do know that they enter a blissful state. This is similar to the athlete in the zone. When the player learns to detach from their past and detach from the noise of the present, they find the zone and begin to win more. The skill of detachment is of great value to athletes who must learn how to defend against energy-draining distractions.

> Mahler's theory of separation and individuation may enable us to shed light on the issue of "detachment." Her theory is one of the most basic paradigms in psychoanalysis (Mahler, 1968), and her model of human development suggests that children go through three stages of development which include fusion with the mother, separation from the mother during the ambulatory stage (2½ years of age) with occasional rapprochement or refueling. Finally, the child is expected to achieve full individuation. With individuation, the child is now said to be detached psychologically and is free to move and think on their own without dependence or interference from the mother. Therefore, individuation and detachment is said to be one of the hallmarks of mental health.

Sport psychologists have tried to use meditation to help athletes to detach from their distractions and enter the zone. Behavioral therapy has been using a variety of meditative techniques for years. Shane Murphy is a sport psychologist working in the US Olympic training facility in Colorado, and in his book, "The Achievement Zone" (Murphy, 1996), he discusses meditative breathing to relax the athlete. The recently developed "acceptance and commitment therapy" advises the patient not to fight off negative thoughts but rather to accept them and let them pass out of the mind, similar to the standard meditation practice which teaches the athlete to continually concentrate on breathing and when thoughts come, simply let them go. Roger Joslin is a marathon runner and an Episcopal cleric. In his book "Running the Spiritual Path," he discusses how to use meditation to run (Joslin, 2003). Tiger Woods was raised Buddhist and has used meditation his entire life. His ability to separate and remain detached is remarkable.

Case Study: This is a 42-year-old amateur tennis player who I had been working with for a number of years. We had gained considerable insights into his performance woes, which centered upon having narcissistic parents who failed to give him any attunement. We came to understand that he had a compulsive need to achieve greatness in order to feel validated. Yet, despite these insights and despite his considerable talent, he still was subject to overwhelming and distracting anxiety during play. He sought out the services of an instructor of Transcendental Meditation who worked with him for a few weeks, teaching him the proper way to meditate and free his mind of clutter. This proved to be a very useful plan of action and he began to use this prior to playing in tennis events. He reported to me that he felt more relaxed and was able to maintain this sense of calm detachment for long periods as he played. However, within a few weeks, he resorted to his old way of worry. It seems reasonable to suggest that for meditation to be effective, one must continue to work with the three jewels of Buddhism; (1) the guru, (2) the practice of meditation and (3) the community of likeminded spirits. Just doing meditation for a few weeks is not enough. This must be done within a community, with a spiritual leader and with a full commitment over an extended period. In this way, proper use of meditation is like the proper use of depth sport psychology. It must be done with a qualified analyst, over an extended period and with adherence to the rules of therapy.

Despite the Freudian perspective that religion is little more than a neurotic fantasy, there can be no doubt that aspects of religious practice can be of help to the anxious or stressed athlete. In this chapter, we observed how the general goal of detachment is shared by Buddhists and those in quest of the athletic zone. In addition, we saw how meditation, if practiced wisely, well and over time, can facilitate feelings of calmness, quietness and peace.

Key Points

- The athlete's quest for the zone and the Buddhist's desire for nirvana share characteristics including detachment, serenity and focus.
- In order to become detached, one must be willing to separate from the world.
- As with anything else, for meditation to work, it must be done under the guidance of an expert, it must be done consistently and it must be supported by others.

Reflective Questions

- Why do clerics from all religious denominations recommend and use prayer?
- Do you still practice prayer and if so when and why?
- Do you think prayer can help the athlete to find peace, calmness and poise?

Exercise Drills for Best Performance

- To practice meditation, one must find a quiet place, do it regularly and be taught how to do it by an expert.
- Each day before a game, take time to sit alone, close your eyes and choose your favorite prayer to recite. Before you do so, breathe deeply and say to yourself that the prayer will help you stay calm and bring you good fortune.

Tips for Best Performance

To practice meditation, one must find a quiet place to do so, one must do it regularly and one must be taught how to do it by an expert.

Recommended Viewing

The South Korean film "Why Has Bodhi Dharma Left for the East" by Bae Yang-Kyun (1989) reflects the detached lifestyle well. It is a film about three Buddhist monks who live an austere contemplative monastic life away from the hustle and bustle of the modern world.

Recommended Reading

Also, "Eat, Pray, Love" by Elizabeth Gilbert is the wonderful true story of how the author left her normal life behind for a year and traveled to Italy, India and then Bali in search of happiness. The challenges she faced when trying to meditate in an ashram in India was a remarkable description of just how tough it is to meditate. It is like a modern-day version of "Walden" but with pasta, pizza and gelato added.

References

Csikszentmihalyi, M. (1990) *Flow*. Harper Collins.
Gorkum, N. (1996) *Buddhism in Daily Life*. Triple Gem Press.

Joslin, R. (2003) *Running the Spiritual Path; A Runner's Guide to Breathing, Meditating and Exploring the Prayful Dimension of the Sport.* St. Martin's Griffin.

Kaminoff, R. & Proshansky, H. (1982) Stress as a Consequence of the Urban Physical Environment. In *Handbook of Stress: Theoretical and Clinical Aspects* (Eds. L. Goldberger & S. Breznitz). Collier Macmillan Publishers, 380–409.

Mahler, M. (1968) *On Human Symbiosis and the Vicissitudes of Individuation Vol. 1.* International Universities Press.

Murphy, S. (1996) *The Achievement Zone: 8 Skills for Winning All the Time from the Playing Field to the Boardroom.* G.P. Putnam's and Sons.

35 Using a "Higher Power" as a Coping Mechanism in Sports

Before stepping into the batter's box, players will often make the sign of the cross. If they hit a home run, you will see them cross home plate, look heavenward and throw a kiss. When a jockey wins the Kentucky Derby, they will point to heaven and smile. These are all demonstrations that the athlete has an active relationship with some higher being lodged above them. Athletes are faced with intense stress, so it's no surprise that they reach for a higher power to find comfort, safety, luck and protection. Some turn to drugs for comfort, others to sex and others to a god. Of the three, choosing to believe in a higher power is the least harmful of these maneuvers. Let us take some time to explore the way athletes introject and use their connection with their god as a way to find shelter from the storm.

According to the 2014 report by the Pew Research Center Forum on Religion and Public Life, approximately 85% of the world population identifies with a religion and have belief in a higher power. The fact that I will be attempting to analyze the psychological mechanisms involved in this form of belief system isn't meant to demean its value or its power. Whether the god is called Zeus, Yahweh, Buddha, Christ or Mohammed, the use of a god to instill humans with strength, good luck, karma, protection, anxiety relief or gratitude has been around for at least 4,000 years and probably more (Bahm, 1994). The psychological defense mechanism used in order to internalize this form of belief is called introjection. Anna Freud suggested that the defense of introjection occurred with the absorption of certain characteristics of a loved one taken in to establish a feeling of control over anxiety or loss (Sandler & Freud, 1985).

> Sigmund Freud's views on religion were harsh and clearly spelled out in "The Future of an Illusion." He wrote "religion is a system of wishful illusion together with a disavowal of reality, such as we find nowhere but in a state of blissful hallucinatory confusion. Religion's eleventh commandment is 'thou shalt not question'" (Freud, 1927).

On the subject of introjection as defense, Anna Freud said introjection is a defense against feelings of helplessness, smallness and impotence.

In order to bolster the self, the person appropriates or introjects qualities of a more powerful entity. Introjection is considered to be an immature defense defined as the internalizing of a love object's characteristics with the goal of establishing closeness to and a constant presence of the object (Meisner, 1985). Sports is filled with anxiety, so it's no great surprise that some turn to a godhead to allay anxiety. The mechanism of introjection in religion is revealed in the ritual of receiving communion with Christ in the Catholic mass. The host is a thin wafer said to represent the body of Christ and when one ingests the host during communion, one is said to incorporate or introject the essence of Christ.

> "Chariots of Fire": The 1981 Academy Award winning film "Chariots of Fire" was the true story about two runners, Eric Liddell and Harold Abrahms. Liddell was a devout Scottish Christian who ran "for the glory of God" and Abrahams, an English Jew, who ran to overcome prejudice. This film highlighted the power of introjection by showing how both men were driven to greatness by a higher power. Liddell used faith in Christ for his inspiration and Abrahams used the more secular figure of Sam Mussabini, his running coach for his inspiration. Mussabini gave Abrahams a medal to wear whereas Liddell wore the cross.

Case Study; on myself: I was an accomplished Division I golfer in college and won tournaments and awards for my college team. After college and graduate school, I joined a golf club and have played in the club championship every year since. Over the years, I also began to write for golf magazines and once did a series on "How I Won My Club Championship" by employing a golf instructor, a physical trainer, buying new equipment and enlisting two clerics to help me out spiritually. To this end, I asked Father Dee McGann, who was a Catholic priest and an elite golfer, and Roger Joslin, a marathon runner, minister and author of the book "Running on the Spiritual Pathway." They both were helpful to me. Roger Joslin taught me contemplative prayer in order to commune with God as I played. He advised me to listen to god's voice as I played a competitive round. I asked him how I would hear him, and he said "God will talk to you in the wind, the air, the clouds and even through the animals as you pass by them on the course." That year as I played in the club championship, I needed a par on number 18 to qualify for the championship flight. I was extremely nervous and as I approached the green, I could see it was surrounded by members watching in interest to see how I would hold up under the pressure. I was terrified with doubt. As I passed by the pond fronting the green, I heard the sound of a frog croaking near the edge of the water, and I recalled what Joslin told me about the voice of God could be heard through the animals. This idea comforted me enough to get down in two putts to qualify. Mission accomplished. Praise the Lord!

One would say that at least temporarily, I had introjected a God into my essence and by committing to the ritual of contemplative prayer and a belief in the support of a higher power as I played, I was sufficiently defended against anxiety. This is a demonstration of how introjection of the love and the comfort of a higher power helped me defensively to cope with my anxiety and enabled me to win.

When that magazine project was completed, it ended my relationship with Roger Joslin and Father Dee McGann and to a large extent so was the introjected power to manage the stress of the championship through a higher power. This is a reminder of the wisdom of Buddhism described in the last chapter. The three tenets of Buddhism include the teaching, the teacher and the community. During my club championship project, I had the teacher, the teachings and the community, but when I terminated my relationship with the priest and the cleric, I still had the teaching of contemplative prayer and I still had the higher power but I no longer had the teacher. This lesson applies to all therapies as well. It takes more than coping tools to manage anxiety. It also takes an ongoing relationship with a therapist.

Key Points

- Belief in a higher power is frequently employed by athletes to cope with anxiety.
- Taking in a belief in a higher power is akin to introjection, the defense defined as internalizing the characteristics of a loved one.
- Freud considered religion to be nothing more than a childish illusion.
- The film "Chariots of Fire" contrasted the way two Olympic sprinters differed in their use of religion to help them run.

Reflective Questions

- Is there any truth in the saying "There are no atheists in foxholes."
- How would you define the concept of God?
- In your view, is the universe a kind, a hostile or a neutral place?
- When do you employ your belief in a higher power?

Exercise Drills for Best Performance

Prayer and meditation can be quite effective if you buy into the belief system, internalize the belief in a higher power, adopt an attitude of forgiveness and self-love. All if this can be facilitated with a connection with a cleric, rabbi or priest on a regular basis. There is no such thing as a magic pill or a magic prayer. Coping with anxiety can come in many forms and coping through a belief in God requires effort, faith, guidance and support.

Tips for Best Performance

Prayer and meditation can be effective but only if you buy into the belief system, can internalize the belief in a higher power and connect with a cleric, rabbi or priest on a regular basis. In other words, there is no such things as a magic pill. Coping with anxiety can come in many forms but coping well requires ongoing work.

Recommended Viewing

The 1981 British historical sport drama "Chariots of Fire" was based upon the true story of two British sprinters in the 1924 Olympics. This film won four Academy Awards and was about the way two different athletes approached their sport, one by using religion and God and the other by using a professional trainer from Italy.

References

Bahm, A. (1994) *The World's Living Religions; A Searching Comparison of the Faiths of East and West*. Jain Publishing Company.

Freud, S. (1927) *The Future of an Illusion* (trans. W.D. Robson-Scott). Hogarth Press.

Religious book

Meisner, W. (1985) Theories of Personality and Psychopathology: Classical Psychoanalysis. In *Comprehensive Textbook of Psychiatry/IV*. Vol 1. (Eds. H. Kaplan & B. Sadock). Williams and Wilkins, 337–418.

Sandler, J. & Freud, A. (1985) Discussion in the Hampstead Index of the Ego and the Mechanisms of Defense. In *Defense and Resistance; Historical Perspective and Current Concepts* (Ed. H. Blum). International Universities Press, 19–146.

36 Mental Health versus Mental Illness in Athletes

The public collapse of sport superstars Naomi Osaka and Simone Biles has fueled the growing concern about the state of mental health in athletes. News of Michael Phelp's depression, headlines of Mike Tyson and Kobe Bryant being accused of rape and NFL players being arrested for domestic violence suggest star athletes may not be the paragons of mental health that we once thought. The publication of *Routledge Handbook of Mental Health in Elite Sport* (2023) addresses the serious mental illness concerns in elite-level competitive sports. Research now suggests that the prevalence of depression and anxiety in athletes is equal if not greater than in the general population (Moesch et al., 2018).

> The World Health Organization's statement concerning mental health and mental illness is as follows:

Mental health is a state of well-being, in which an individual realizes his or her own abilities, can cope with the normal stresses of life, can work productively and is able to make a contribution to his or her community. Mental disorders represent disturbances to a person's mental health that are often characterized by some combination of troubled thoughts, emotions, behavior and relationships with others. Examples of mental disorders include depression, anxiety disorder, conduct disorder, bipolar disorder and psychosis.

The question is how best to treat the athlete who suffers this way. Over the last century, there has been three major approaches to the treatment of mental illness, including psychoanalysis, psychopharmacology and behaviorism. Psychoanalysis is based upon Freud's work with the unconscious, psychopharmacology uses medicine to treat symptoms and behaviorism began with the classical and operant conditioning research of Pavlov

(1927) and Skinner (1965) and later included a cognitive approach (Ellis & Dryden, 2007). Anyone familiar with sport psychology understands that the field uses a cognitive/behavioral approach given the stated promise of rapid recovery. However, as Dalal clearly pointed out (Dalal, 2018), the stated promise of a quick fix is more a myth than a reality. Nonetheless, the dominance of the cognitive/behavioral approach to athletes remains and this has resulted in a field which cannot deliver on this promise. This does damage to the field's name and reputation.

Some could argue that the field of psychology has spent the last 120 years running away from Sigmund Freud's discovery of the unconscious. The field of psychiatry embraced pharmacology as a quick way to repress anxiety and depression and this left any real verbal treatment of mental illness to psychologists and social workers. By mid-20th century, behaviorism ascended as the preferred treatment of choice, systematically denying the existence of the unconscious and casting aspersions at the talking cure. Both psychopharmacology and behaviorism represent flights into mental health and have given birth to positive psychology which can be summed up with the phrase "don't worry, be happy." Major contributors to the field of positive psychology include Martin Seligman (1998). It is ironic that Seligman's basic and elegant research was based upon the concept of learned helplessness with dogs but turned his attention away from the concept of helplessness and instead defensively focused upon optimism and happiness.

It is my belief that any real gains in mental health of the athlete must involve a psychodynamic approach which is designed to penetrate, explore and resolve the underlying, unconscious causes of self-defeat, performance problems, personality disorders and symptom formation. The following case will explore the underlying dynamics of an elite athlete in order to demonstrate the complex nature of the athlete's mind and how to deal with it.

Case Study

The following case demonstrates the connection between performance anxiety in a pitcher with mental illness issues and how mental illness issues can be exacerbated by the competitive sports environment. There is no escape from childhood issues nor is it easy to deal with the hypercompetitive sports culture. Both internal and external factors can be extreme and career ending as we saw in the case of Naomi Osaka, Simone Biles and Mike Tyson.

This athlete came to me during his first year at college where he was a full scholarship Division I golfer who suffered with putting and chipping yips, an anxiety-based spasm occurring during the swing. His demeanor was somewhat guarded and his concerns focused on his yips and his general anxiety. He had chronic ambivalence about golf which stemmed back to childhood. As a latency age child, he had little interest in sports and was a solitary cerebral child who spent endless hours building Lego sets or tinkering with his computer. However, his dad encouraged him to play golf, and to please the father, this youngster quickly became a star on the AGJI national tour. The social recognition he gained as a star golfer compelled him to continue to play despite the pressure and abuse felt from his coaches, the coercion he felt from his father and the loss of his true interests in building things. He described his experience of being of a nationally ranked golfer as "a big waste of time." He continued to play and was willing to work hard and to live up to the perfectionistic demands of his coaches which led him into habits of overwork and burnout. In addition, he developed an obsession with gaining weight since he had a small thin frame and his coach encouraged bigness.

I taught him standard behavioral interventions to help him to relax and control his anxiety while putting and this had minor to moderate effectiveness. Against my advice, he terminated the work within ten sessions, and I assumed I would never see him again. However, within six months, he returned with reports of depression and anxiety. In the interim, he had quit the golf team and felt depressed. The loss of his golf career became the next major topic of analysis in his once weekly sessions. With the loss of golf, his demeanor changed subtly and he presented as a bit more withdrawn and angrier. However, he flourished in his academics, and upon graduation, he landed a job in the finance world.

With regards to his underlying depression, we can observe the accumulation of losses that he had endured as he became deeply involved with his sport. He had already given up on his childhood habits, and now, he experienced the loss of his golf career which had offered him some measure of fame and accolades. Without a working through of these multiple losses, the athlete will be prone to a repetition compulsion or the repeating of his pattern of compliance and resentment.

> Freud on repetition compulsions: The repetition compulsion is the unconscious tendency to repeat a traumatic event by putting yourself in a setting which guarantees this will happen again. Freud suggested that this was our unconscious way of trying to master a past trauma but that we do this without awareness of what we are doing (Freud, 1914). This explains why people who were abused as kids wind up marrying an abusive spouse. In the case under discussion here, the athlete appeared to find himself in situations where he was frustrated, felt he was being forced into doing what he did not want to do and was angry about it.

His job in finance revealed a familiar pattern where he felt resentful of having to do things he did not enjoy doing similar to his childhood when he wanted to spend time experiencing the creative and aesthetic pleasure of building Legos but was pulled out of this private world and coerced into playing golf. Now, in his corporate job, he felt a similar conflict. He preferred to work in the area of research analysis but instead was put on a sales desk. This once again led to burnout and anger as he harbored resentment to the company that he was never able to do what he preferred to do. His past patterns of emotions, perceptions and behaviors were repeating themselves. His earliest experience of not getting to do what he loved to do was now playing out in an entirely different setting. But now the consequences of this conflict were different. In golf, he initially manifested the anger about the conflict through chipping yips and then by quitting. As an adult, he would not be yipping but rather he began to think about quitting this high-paying job. Entire months were spent debating whether he should quit his job or stay. In cases like this, I have seen that a failure to discuss the inner dynamics will lead to a self-defeating acting out of the conflict.

This case began with the seemingly commonplace issue of short game yips but in fact that symptom represented a conflict about doing what he felt he was forced into rather than doing what he liked to do as a child. This conflict manifested with skewed perceptions, distorted thinking and compulsive behaviors all stemming from unconscious and unresolved dynamics that occurred during latency age. This is an ongoing case where we try to ensure that he does not act out his repetition compulsions by quitting his job based upon dynamics that he knows little about. Insight is hard earned, but there is a large payoff in mood, stability and economic security.

I presented this case to demonstrate the way performance issues are a manifestation of deeper mental health concerns and that the dynamics of the case require that one be able to understand the internal workings of the athlete in order to help them get free from unresolved and burdensome issues and to escape from blindly repeating a life of self-defeat and sadness.

Key Points

- There is a current crisis of mental health in athletes today given the hypercompetitive nature of the sport's culture and the failure of sport psychology to address this.
- Standard cognitive/behavioral interventions are not designed to address the deeper issues that many elite athletes deal with.
- The use of psychopharmacology to deal with the athletes' mental health concerns often produces troublesome side effects such as weight gain or slowed reaction time.

Reflective Questions

- What is it about sports that creates so much stress in the athlete?
- Name three things that produce chronic anxiety in the famous athlete.
- How does the athlete balance the need to excel with the need to be self-accepting of failure?

Exercise Drills for Best Performance

If one is troubled with chronic anxiety, depression or a slump, it is probably wise to seek out professional help with a trained psychoanalyst, especially if you have already tried behavioral mental skills training. Often times, the environment of sports demands excellence and many coaches exacerbate this dynamic. The result is as psychological collapse during the teen years where the young talented athlete often does not have strong enough defense to cope with this kind of pressure. To avoid mental breakdowns and quitting the sport you once loved, find yourself a good therapist to work on your defenses.

> ### Tips for Best Performance
>
> If one is troubled with chronic anxiety, depression or patterns of self-defeat, it is probably wise to seek out professional help with a trained psychoanalyst, especially if you have already tried behavioral mental skills training.

Recommended Reading

"Unpacking Depth Sport Psychology: Cases Studies in the Unconscious" by Tom Ferraro.

References

Dalal, F. (2018) *CBT: The Cognitive Behavioral Tsunami; Managerialism, Politics and the Corruptions of Science*. Routledge.

Ellis, A. & Dryden, W. (2007) *The Practice of Rational Emotive Behavior Therapy*. 2nd edition. Springer Publishing Company.

Freud, S. (1914) Remembering, Repeating and Working Through. In *The Standard Edition of the Complete Works of Sigmund Freud* Vol. 12 (trans. James Strachey). Hogarth, 145–156.

Moesch, K., Kentta, G., Kleinart, J., Quignon-Fleuret, C., Cecil, S., & Bertollo, M. (2018) FEPSAC Position Statement: Mental Health Disorders in Elite Athletes and Models of Service Provision. *Psychology of Sport and Exercise*, 38: 61–71.

Nixdorf, I., Nixdorf, R., & MacIntyre, T., (2023) Mental Health in Athletes. In *Routledge Handbook of Mental Health in Elite Sport* (Eds. I. Nixdorf, R. Nixdorf, J. Beckmann, S. Martin, & T. MacIntyre). Routledge, 3–11.
Pavlov, I. (1927) *Conditioned Reflexes*. Oxford University Press.
Seligman, M. (1998) *Learned Optimism*. Pocket Books.
Skinner, B.F. (1965) *Science and Human Behavior*. Free Press.

37 The Problem of Prescription Drug Use in Athletes

Although not ordinarily included on a list of defense mechanisms, the desire for medication is frequently a sign of resistance and used as a defense against further growth or therapeutic connection. When medication is obtained, it will often interrupt the work of insight and why it can be considered a basic defense used by athletes. The medication defense is similar to acting out by missing appointments or by requesting that the sessions be cut down from weekly to every other week. The request for antidepressants is usually made when progress is felt and the athlete becomes vaguely aware that they are growing dependent on a therapist they like. This is frightening to many athletes and rather than face the prospect of dependency, growth and loss of control, they make a request for medication with an unconscious hope that dependency on a drug will be far better than dependency on the therapist.

Leon Wurmser's landmark work with compulsive drug users (1978) hypothesizes that the compulsive drug user enlists the primitive defenses of avoidance, dissociation and acting out. Requests for an antidepressant can sometimes be seen as an act of avoidance employed to divert attention away from therapeutic and/or psychological growth. Salzman talks at length about the obsessive patients' defensive embrace of pseudo-independence in order to maintain the illusion of omniscient power. The obsessive believes this can be done through medication (Salzman, 1985).

In cases of psychotic depression or severe depression which is accompanied by agitation, poor sleep, loss of appetite, anhedonia, lethargy, guilt and suicidality, the short-term use of either electroconvulsive therapy or antidepressants is needed. But in most cases, we are not facing psychotic or major depression but rather dysthymia with its familiar constellation of persistent symptoms, including self-doubt, sadness, anxiety, low self-esteem and insomnia.

The following is a typical case of a request for antidepressants as defense against therapeutic progress.

This is a 13-year-old nationally ranked golfer who was playing below potential and showing signs of anxiety, self-defeat and self-consciousness. He was functioning adequately academically.

Our work focused on his performance anxiety and its causes. His father was overly involved and was extremely aggressive which meant that the son would frequently witness the father getting into many highly volatile and embarrassing verbal altercations with a variety of people on the road or at golf matches.

After about 1½ years of weekly sessions, his golf began to improve dramatically and he became a national presence. However, as competitive pressure mounted, he began to feel more anxiety and the father began to suggest that he might need an antidepressant to help control focus, anxiety and anger which now was becoming evident on the course. I commented that medication may be some relief but the negative side effects of slower reaction time, weaker focus and less energy far outweighed the positive ones. Gary Wadler's book "Drugs and the Athlete" (1989) provides more support for this as he concludes there is virtually no evidence that athletic performance can be improved with any drug.

This parent would not be deterred and took his son to another doctor who provided the drug requested. He began to cut down his sessions to every other week. Over the next three months, the player became angrier, shouting and pouting on the course when mistakes occurred and began to brutally smack his thigh whenever he made a mistake which caused visible bruising. At this point, the father took him back to the doctor and requested an increase in the dosage of the antidepressant.

The underlying and unresolved pool of anger in the player was now being unleashed as the antidepressant loosened her naturally established defenses. The player's anger was derived partially from the father's abuse and partially from the increased pressure felt at this new level of competition and partially as resistance to his growing dependency and appreciation of me. Drug intake, whether prescribed or from the street, may temporarily suppress the immediate emotional issues but these emotions must still be faced and coped with. The more antidepressants he took, the more weight he gained, the more lethargy he felt and the less strategic and slower were his reaction times. These are all the standard side effects with antidepressants and when used by high-level elite athletes, the consequence is a decline in ranking and performance.

This case reveals the way athletes will try to avoid the anxiety and increased helplessness induced by moving up in rank and by moving into deeper dependency and appreciation of the therapist. And in the treatment of the young athlete, one also sees the jealousy and loss felt by the parent who observes the youngster's growing attachment to the therapist. In these cases, the parent is encouraging the use of antidepressants. Taking of antidepressants may serve to reduce anxiety temporarily and they are better than turning to street drugs, but one can expect negative side effects, a stalling of therapeutic progress and a flattening of performance.

Key Points

- The request for antidepressants may be a way the athlete is attempting to avoid the painful work of psychotherapy.
- There is little proof that antidepressants will aid on the field performance.
- Standard side effects of antidepressants include weight gain and slower reaction time.
- Taking of any drug may disrupt the well-established defenses that are functioning to repress underlying emotions.

Reflective Questions

- Why do you think athletes take drugs or ask for medication?
- If you have taken an antidepressant, have you noticed any side effects?
- How would you manage a patient who asked for either a stimulant or an antidepressant?

Exercise Drills for Best Performance

- Drill #1: It is best to exercise patience and outline both the benefits and negative side effects of prescription medication. One will often see the obsessional athlete who disdains human connection ask for drugs in order to maintain a pseudo-independence. It is often necessary to face, discuss and understand underlying emotional turmoil and unconscious conflicts if you hope to have lasting improvement.

> Tips for Best Performance
>
> It is best to exercise patience with regard to athletic progress and not rush toward an embrace of prescription drug use as an easy answer. It is often necessary to face, discuss and understand underlying emotional turmoil if you hope to have lasting improvement.

Further Reading

Leon Wurmser's *The Hidden Dimension: Psychodynamics in Compulsive Drug Use*. Jason Aronson.

References

Salzman, L. (1985) *Treatment of the Obsessive Personality*. Jason Aronson.
Wadler, G. & Hainline, B. (1989) *Drugs and the Athlete*. F.A. Davis Company.
Wurmser, L. (1978) *The Hidden Dimension, Psychodynamics in Compulsive Drug Use*. Jason Aronson.

38 Depression Used as a Defense by Athletes Who Fear Failure

Defenses can be used to avoid anxious memories but they also can be used to avoid anxious events of the future. Some athletes use depression, apathy and negativity to avoid upcoming anxiety they feel ill-equipped to handle. This kind of defense is manifested through negativity, flat affect, pessimism, a lack of energy and passivity like character armor used to defend against feelings of anxiousness of success. All neurosis has secondary gain which means it has a benefit. This is what we mean by fear of success, a subject Freud wrote about in his essay "Those Wrecked by Success" (1916).

The psychoanalyst Edward Bibring explored the manner in which apathetic depression acts as a defense, protecting the person from future intolerable losses (1953). When this defense occurs in the sporting arena, you have a player who lacks energy, drive and spontaneity. They look lethargic and can't take the shot. Bibring suggests that depression and apathy can be used to avoid risk taking and the threat of failure.

Kirschner (1985) synthesizes some of Bibring's ideas and suggested an avoidance of risk can become a characteristic pattern of defense aimed at preserving self-esteem. I have treated athletes who take the "safe route" as they play, thinking that not taking a shot is better than taking one and missing. I will describe three athletes, two baseball players and a basketball player whose fear of loss translated into the embrace of mediocrity with its familiar failure to take risks and a flat emotionless demeanor.

Case #1: This 16-year-old elite high school soccer player was brought in by his parents who described him as perfectionistic and having lost confidence. His demeanor was flat, he lacked enthusiasm and was generally pessimistic in his approach to life. He was a good student and had an impressive sports career, and it was generally expected that he would be recruited to play Division I soccer in college. In his freshman year in high school, he played on varsity as a striker and won the MVP award. He was a standout player on his highly ranked travel team. His anxiety and worry emerged at the beginning of his sophomore year after he showed a slight decline in his scoring statistics. This led him to try to win a kicking contest prior to being warmed up which caused a minor tear in his hamstring. This led to an overall sense of defeat, lack of motivation to return to soccer and discussion of whether he ought to quit. When we elaborated on his lack of motivation, he admitted that he was afraid to return to soccer because he did not want to re-experience anxiety on the field under the weight of expectations. His dynamic demonstrated Bibring's theory of how people use depression to avoid future risk of failure. This athlete was showing signs of apathy, depression, lack of motivation and a wish to quit the sport he once loved out of a defense against re-experiencing overwhelming pressure to perform.

Case #2: This Division I baseball player was demanding and perfectionistic and felt as if he was in a slump in college. He had flat affect and was unresponsive emotionally to any topic of discussion. He was robotic, depersonalized and bored. However, when we began to explore the history of his problems, he reported that he was always tired, lacked enthusiasm for all things, had a poor appetite and poor sleep, all characteristics of depression. When I asked him how long he suffered this way, he said since 6th grade when his family moved from the Dominican Republic to the United States. His father's job forced him to stay in the Dominican Republic but the rest of the family, including my patient, moved to New York. This loss of his friendships, home, father and school was overwhelming to him and he was not able to receive solace from his mother who herself was anxious and depressed over the move. This set up a defense pattern of withdrawal, avoidance of affect and avoidance of any further losses, even if that occurred in baseball, a sport he had always excelled at. His perfectionism led him to feel inappropriate anxiety whenever he made a mistake, and based upon his history of unresolved loss in childhood, he developed the defense of depression, avoidance, apathy and lack of motivation.

Case #3: This 35-year-old computer designer was a former standout high school golfer. He had an overinvolved and demanding and impossible to please father who was a scratch golfer himself and coached him throughout his childhood. The father's continuous criticism diminished the patient's self-image, making it impossible for him to manage competitive anxiety. All of this came to a head prior to County Championships in his junior year. During pregame warmups supervised by the father, the patient experienced a panic attack and went on to play defensively during the tournament and thereafter became an unremarkable, defensive golfer. His swing grew tense and his strategies were too defensive. In his personal life, during high school, he had been dating a pretty girl who he broke up with out of fear he would never be able to live up to her expectations. He quit golf prior to entering college. However, his avoidant risk-averse stance followed him into his career. He had considerable talent as a computer designer and landed a position with a global technology company.

Over time, he seemed to embrace mediocrity in order to avoid further risk, failure and promotion. This defense of passivity and risk avoidance apparently became entrenched in his character and infiltrated all areas of his life, including his love life and his career. He functioned as a good team player who could execute instructions well but lacked any creative initiative, which was an essential part of his work as a computer designer. He chronically avoided any creative or assertive behaviors and he deeply feared a promotion because it would mean he would have to make decisions that may fail. He was developmentally stuck with the defense of depression, passivity, negativity and weakness to avoid the risky world of success. This lack of initiative referred back to his fear of hitting golf shots. As this defense became more conscious, we came to see that his fragile and undeveloped ego needed support. Over time, as his insight grew and as his confidence and self-worth were bolstered, he gained greater voice and was able to take more risks, face up to pressuring situations and withstand the anxiety of growth. This is a former athlete turned employee and we continue to work on this unconscious defense and replace it with assertiveness and self-esteem.

Key Points

- Unresolved losses can produce a character trait of risk avoidance and passivity.
- In sports, the athlete who looks apathetic, passive and performs without passion may be using depression as defense.
- It is necessary to help these athletes to see the genesis of their passivity and avoidant nature.

Reflective Questions

- Why do you think some athletes are so afraid to take a risk?
- Some athletes will use procrastination to avoid growth. Do you know anyone like this?
- Describe the look of an athlete who is passive and avoiding the pace of play on the field.

Exercise Drills for Best Performance

- Drill #1: If you coach a player who seems to be avoidant and keeps passing the ball rather than shooting, this may be a case of an athlete who is deathly afraid to fail. Many athletes tell me they fear that one mistake prompts the coach to bench them, and rather than risk the shame of being benched, they avoid shooting altogether. This can produce a failed season for the entire team. The coach needs to be aware of this damaging fear and have some locker room talks to explain that being benched is not a punishment but instead it gives the player a chance to rest. Let them talk a bit about their fear of mistakes and address it with them. Perhaps, the best thing that ever happened to the New York Yankees was when George Steinbrenner hired Joe Torre. What Torre did was to protect his players from the wrath vented by Steinbrenner which then freed the team up and produced a winning dynasty which included Derek Jeter and Alex Rodriguez.

Tips for Best Performance

If a player you coach is apathetic, listless and seems to lack motivation, it may be that they have a masked depression. It is best to have a talk with him about what they are troubled by, and if it seems they have experienced a loss that remains unresolved, you should recommend they be seen by a competent psychotherapist.

Further Reading

An excellent volume about depression, including masked depression, is edited by Vamik Volkan (1985) titled *Depressive States and Their Treatment* published by Jason Aronson.

References

Bibring, E. (1933) The Mechanism of Depression. In *Affective Disorders; Psychoanalytic Contributions to Their Study* (Ed. P. Greenacre). International Universities Press, 13–48.
Freud, S. (1916) *Thise Wrecked by Success*. Some Character-Types Met With in Psycho-analytic Work (trans. J. Strachey). Hogarth Press.
Kirschner, (1985) The Depressive Process Examined in View of Creativity. In *Depressive States and Their Treatment* (Ed. V. Volkan). Jason Aronson, 71–94.

39 Cultural Differences in the Use of Defenses

The sports world is increasingly global in nature which provides ample opportunity to learn performance strategies from foreign countries. When an MLB player for the Dominican Republic makes the sign of the cross before they get into the batter's box, they are using a belief in a higher power as a defense and to bring good fortune. Many do this and many players from the Dominican Republic do well in the MLB.

Women golfers from South Korea now dominate the LPGA, a game that requires one to suppress almost all emotions. South Korean women are able to do this. Can suppression be taught to help others cope with anxiety? As globalization of sport continues, multiculturalism will bring performance strategies that will be shared and defense strategies that may trump all other secrets. The book "Mental Health in Elite Sport: Applied Perspectives from Across the Globe" is a beginning effort to explore the psychological differences in athletes from different parts of the world (Larsen et al., 2021).

In this chapter, we will look at global differences in the use of defense mechanisms. Learning better defenses that foreign players unconsciously use has the potential to make any team dominant. Teams regularly hire coaches from other nations in order to learn new strategies and attitudes. However, it is a big assumption to say that these coaches are aware of how their nation's athletes employ their defense mechanisms. Let us look at a few of the more salient defenses used by athletes from Europe, South Korea, Brazil, Mexico, Japan, Thailand and America. We can gain guidance by reviewing the literature on culture-bound syndromes (Lewis-Fernandez et al., 2009) and many of these culture-bound syndromes are now included in DSM V.

Examples of culture-bound syndromes include "Nervios," a term for distress among Latinos and consisting of shouting, crying, headaches, irritability, trembling, nervousness and sleep problems. "Amok" is a dissociative syndrome seen in Malaysia and the Philippines and includes outbursts of violent, aggressive or homicidal behavior. "Hwa-byung" is a Korean anger syndrome with symptoms that include insomnia, fatigue, indigestion and general aches and pains. Culture-bound syndromes focus on pathology but researchers are yet to explore the differences in coping skills or defense mechanisms which are a form of adaptation. However, Nixdorf et al.'s (2023) work has an international flavor by using Keyes' two-dimensional model which attempts to connect mental illness paradigms with mental health paradigms but these researchers make little use of the paradigm of defense mechanisms.

Let us choose several nations and explore how athletes from these countries employ their characteristic defenses.

The European Athletes' Use of Altruism: Altruism is defined as the tendency to deal with external stress by dedication to the needs of others. This allows one to satisfy attachment needs and to feel good by helping another. A friend of mine runs a major international company and has the chance to play in pro-ams both with European golfing stars and American golfers of equal fame. He often plays in the Alfred Dunhill Links Championship at St, Andrews which draws the biggest names in European golf. He has described the way European players go out of their way to help him. Padrick Harrington of Ireland provided him with a 15-minute putting lesson and Martin Kaymer of Germany gave him a 15-minute chipping lesson. He was hitting shots next to Jose Maria Olazabal on the range and Olazabal accidently hit some dirt onto my friend's jacket. Jose ran over to him, apologized profusely and offered to buy him a new jacket. These incidents all reveal the trait of altruism on the part of these European superstars. However, his experiences playing in American Pro-ams with American superstars is quite a different story. He told me that when he played a round with one American superstar, the player barely said a word all day, but instead sat in his own golf cart by himself and looked at his cell phone all round long. This story is a good example of the character of the European golfers who present as more humble, generous and kind and show the defense of altruism.

Mexican and Hispanic athletes and the use of humor and affiliation: Perhaps, the funniest player ever to walk the links was Lee Trevino, the Mexican golfer called "The Merry Mex." He had a remarkable ability to joke around and play pranks on others no matter how big the event. His most famous prank came at the U.S. Open at Merion Golf Club on the first tee prior to an 18 hole playoff against Jack Nicklaus. He had a rubber snake in his bag and threw it at Jack Nicklaus to playfully startle him. This was met with great amusement and laughter in the crowd, but as it turned out, it may have been an effective use of humor as an icebreaker since "The Merry Mex," who was the clear underdog, went on to win that day and take home the U.S. Open trophy. Another Hispanic golfer with an endearing sense of humor was Puerto Rican golf star Chi-Chi Rodriguez whose clever antics always delighted crowds. In a way, he always had home court advantage, thanks to his charming funny banter which contrasted sharply with the cool, arrogant, even narcissistic attitude of the typical American golfers he was paired with. The use of humor as an adaptive high-level defense mechanism requires high-level intelligence and a desire to connect with others. The film superstar and standup comedian John Leguizamo was born in Columbia and is another good example of Hispanic humor and likability.

AFFILIATION: Affiliation is a highly adaptive defense of dealing with internal or external stress by turning to others for support. This allows for the expression of feelings, reduces the feeling of isolation and enhances the chances of gathering new ways to cope. The Hispanic cultural value of "personalismo" or personalism is the desire to reach full potential through positive nurturing relationships. One of my patients is a Division I baseball player who is Mexican American. He told that throughout his baseball career he has seen a marked difference between Mexican teammates and his American teammates. He told me that the Mexican players were more lighthearted, would joke around more and tended to be more relaxed overall. In contrast, he said that his American teammates were more highly stressed, tensed and uptight. The Mexican value of personalism is clearly seen in the film "Roma" by Mexican filmmaker Alejandro Inarritu. This film demonstrated the strong bonds felt within a family. Another Hispanic superstar was Sammy Sosa who became world famous in 1998 as he vied with Mark McGwire in pursuit of Roger Maris's single season home run record. Sammy Sosa was Dominican-American and I recall the way he was largely ignored by the American press who seemed to marginalize and discount him but instead sided with American Mark McGwire (Ferraro, 1998).

The Hispanic use of humor and their affiliative capacity are two valuable defenses that other athletes can learn from.

How South Korean female athletes use suppression to cope with anxiety: As noted above, South Korean women have had a significant presence on the LPGA since the arrival of Se-ri Pak and her U.S. Open victory in 1998. There have been many articles written about the Korean wave on the LPGA over the last twenty years. Their domination is partly due to their work ethic, their family support but their success on tour is also due to their ability to suppress emotions. Suppression is the ability to temporarily and intentionally avoid thinking about a disturbing or overwhelming problem, desire, or feeling. This defense is evident by observing the unflappable, cool demeanor of the South Korean golfers as they finish off a tournament. No sign of stress, anxiety or anger is ever seen. There is a long history of emotional control in Korea especially for women. They have been trained not to make noise, not to laugh and not to be boisterous in any way. This is why you will often see South Korean women cover their mouths when they laugh as they try to suppress their laughter. An example of how South Koreans learn to suppress is seen in the following case. I was treating a 18-year-old female golfer from South Korea and we were at a professional golf event that she had qualified for. As she was warming up on the range, she said to me that her back was hurting badly. Since there were some chiropractors working in this event, I went up to the golfer's father and told him that his daughter's back was hurting and that maybe she should get an adjustment from one of the chiropractors there. He immediately said to me "NO, my daughter does not have any back pain." Rest assured, this stoic response on the part of the father had been communicated many times in the past and eventually the child learns to suppress and disregard these unpleasant feelings. This uncomplaining, suppressed Stoic attitude instills keen focus in the athlete and strategies can be taught which train other athletes to adopt this way of coping.

Japanese athletes, the kawaii syndrome and reaction formation: Naomi Osaka was the first Japanese player to win a grand slam title, doing so in 2018 at the age of 21. She quickly became one of the most marketable female athletes in the world. She has been described as shy, soft-spoken and averts eye contact and has admitted to dealing with depression for the last 5 years. Her rise to the top was followed by her sudden and dramatic exit from it, announcing her retirement last year due to "personal reasons." She admitted that it had become increasingly difficult to manage fame, press questions and competition. One way to understand her sudden collapse is to refer to what is called "kawaii syndrome" in Japan or the attitude of presenting the self as meek, non-threatening, quiet and passive. The most internationally popular symbols of the "kawaii syndrome" is the fictional character "Hello Kitty," the cute mouthless kitten that has become a global marketing phenomenon currently bringing in over $8 billion per year to Sanrio the company that created this image. In other words, the "kawaii" symbol of cuteness is powerful. The kawaii syndrome has been described in the past by myself and others (Ferraro, 2016) and derives from the unresolved Japanese trauma of the bombing of Hiroshima and Nagasaki which ended World War II. This trauma remains largely unresolved and the way that the Japanese have tried to get beyond this trauma is by employing the reaction formation of passivity. Reaction formation of passivity means that one presents oneself as defenseless, harmless and cute in order to avoid provoking attack against you. One can see that this is a problematic defense for athletes who need to be in touch with their aggression in order to win. Osaka has frequently admitted (Video) that she has to suppress all of her instinctive nature in order to present a "nice girl" public persona. I think the nature of this cultural defense was in such conflict with her need to enlist her aggression that has collapsed her and led to her depression. My research with Japanese sport psychologist Kaori Fukada supports this. When we interviewed Japanese golfers, we discovered they all had trouble discussing the concept of anger and aggression (Ferraro, 2002).

American athletes and self-idealization: Although America is described as a melting pot of different cultures, there are by now discernible characteristics of its citizens. Alexis de Tocqueville may have been the first to outline the American character as practical, busy minded, restless and nonintellectual (de Tocqueville, 1840). He coined the phrase "American Exceptionalism" to describe these traits. Another notable social analysis of the American psyche came from D.H. Lawrence in his essay about Benjamin Franklin (Lawrence, 1923). He concludes the essay by describing the typical American as "productive machines like millions of squirrels running in millions of cages" (p. 27). Today, what Alexis de Tocqueville described as American exceptionalism and compulsive productivity seems to have morphed into self-idealization or grandiosity, the defense of assigning exaggerated greatness to oneself. Clearly, a climate for narcissistic absorption has been in America since the 1970s (Lasch, 1979). America's secret strength is its self-absorption and its sense of grandiosity as McWilliams explained (McWilliams, 1994, p. 169). I could sight many examples of self-idealization in the American athletes I work with. They all need a sense of grandiosity and idealization to withstand the anxiety induced by chronic competition, and this leads to ambition and drive but also to disappointment, anger and severe devaluation as well. One case I had was with a PGA golfer who would expect and insist upon winning every tournament he entered. This attitude led to pressing, overtrying and eventually devaluation. Over many months, he was able to learn that if he won two to three events a year, he would be doing far better than most. It took us at least three years of working on this problem of self-idealization for him to relinquish it. Self-idealization produces drive and great goal-setting, but when taken too far, it can lead to devaluation and a sense of failure and depression.

Argentine soccer fans use macho as a reaction formation against homosexuality. Soccer is the world's favorite spectator sport and produces intense and passionate fan participation, as well as fan violence and hooliganism. This is very much the case in South America, the birthplace of Pele and Marta, who many consider to be the best male and female soccer players in history. The South American soccer players use flair, creativity, speed and tenacity and their fans have passion for the game. Harvard professor Marcelo Suarez-Orozco (1999) studied the soccer fixation in Argentina by analyzing the content of the songs the fans would chant as they rooted for their home team. He used Helene Deutsch's (1926) work which explained that males were fascinated with balls games because it allowed them to project themselves into their idols and by so doing master their own masculinity. When Suarez-Orozco analyzed the soccer chants, he realized they were all about sexual conquest with the winners establishing a macho maleness and the losers being converted into females. Words like rape, asses, penetration were used throughout the chants. Suarez-Orozco concluded that the themes of these chants were based upon a fear of being debased into a passive, emasculated role. As he explained, soccer and many other ball games involve men protecting their "end zone" from penetration by the aggressive rival. The defensive dynamic of reaction formation against passivity is seen in many sports (Sachs, 1984). Using sport as a reaction formation against passivity means that the male is unconsciously anxious about his masculinity. There is a current "boy's crisis" in America with college enrollment for boys declining steadily. It is reasonable to note that sports will continue to be a way that boys and men can shore up their male identity. Carol Gilligan's feminist classic "In a Different Voice: Psychological Theory and Women's Development" (1982) explained why men's gender identity tends to be so rigid and easily threatened. The fact that it is easily threatened explains not only the soccer chants heard in Argentina but why sport in general is needed and valued by most men. To suggest that sports are a defense against the male fear of homosexual tendencies may feel like an outrageous claim but as Freud said, the business of revealing what lies within the unconscious is always seen as an unwelcome revelation and a narcissistic blow that will be resisted, feared and denied.

This brief analysis of cultural differences in defense mechanisms should show that as sports become more global, there is much to learn about the differences in athletes from foreign lands.

Key Points

- Sports is increasingly global in nature and we stand to benefit if we can learn how athletes form different nations manage their stress.
- No serious work has been done in an effort to explore the way athletes from different nations use their defenses to manage anxiety.
- A case was made that Hispanics use humor to good effect during competition.
- South Korean women are seen as using suppression to good effect in golf.
- Japanese athletes may be unconsciously using reaction formation in the form of "the kawaii syndrome" as a result of the dropping of the atomic bomb and a fear of provoking further aggression.
- American athletes tend to use self-idealization during play as a nationally learned character trait.
- South American soccer fans well-known macho attitude may be dictated by doubts about masculinity.

Reflective Questions

- What nation are you from and do you think your nation of origin has given you certain traits. If so, what traits?
- Do you think South Koreans are able to suppress their emotions better than most, and if so, why?
- South American men are said to be "macho." What does this mean and do you think it's true?
- Japanese athletes tend to smile and be very gracious. Does this impact their play?

Exercise Drills for Best Performance

- Drill #1: All athletes can learn many things by observing players from other countries. A good drill is to observe a player from another nation play, and then if you can, sit and talk to them about how they play and whether they think their character has been influenced by their country of origin. If you listen carefully, you may be able to adopt a more casual, a more fun loving or a more aggressive stance. This is called role modeling.

Tips for Best Performance

All athletes should be open to learning the approaches taken by players from other countries. There is much to learn from them.

Further Reading

Psychoanalysis and Culture at the Millenium. (1999) Edited by Nancy Ginsburg and Roy Ginsburg. Yale University.

References

De Toqueville, A. (1840) *Democracy in America* (trans. H. Reeves). Saunders and Otley.

Deutsche, H. (1926) Contribution to the Psychology of Sport. *International Journal of Psycho-Analysis*, 7: 223–227.

Ferraro, T. (1998) Race in Baseball Is Not Just for a Pennant. *Newsday Editorial*. Sept., 12th 1998.

Ferraro, T. (2002) Aggression among Athletes: An Asian versus American Comparison. *Athletic Insight*, 1(1), 1–5.

Ferraro, T. (2016) The Japanese Power of Cute. *Alist Magazine*, Fall Edition.

Gilligan, C. (1982) *In a Different Voice: Psychological Theory on Women's Development*. Harvard University Press.

Larson, H., Moesch, K., Durand-Bush, N., & Henriksen, K. (2021) *Mental Health in Elite Sports: Applied Perspectives from Across the Globe*. Routledge.

Lasch, C. (1979) *The Culture of Narcissism*. W. W. Norton and Company.

Lawrence, D.H. (1923) *Studies in Classic American Literature*. Penguin Books.

Lewis-Fernandez, R., Guarnaccia, P., & Ruiz, P. (2009) Culture-Bound Syndromes. In *Kaplan & Sadock's Comprehensive Textbook of Psychiatry*, 9th Edition. Vol. 1 (Eds. B. Sadock, V. Sadock, & P. Ruiz). Lippincott Williams & Wilkins, 2519–2538.

McWilliams, N. (1994) *Psychoanalytic Diagnosis: Understanding Personality Structure in the Clinical Process*. The Guilford Press.

Nixdorf, I., Nixdorf, R., Beckmann, J., Martin, S., & Macintrye, T. (2023) *Routledge Handbook of Mental Health in Elite Sport*. Routledge.

Naomi Osaka film

Sachs, M. (1984) A Psychoanalytic Perspective on Running. In *Running as Therapy; An Integrated Approach*.(Eds. M. Sachs& G. Buffone). University of Nebraska Press, 101–111.

Suarez-Orozco, M. (1999) A Psychoanalytic Study of Argentine Soccer. In *Psychoanalysis & Culture at the Millennium* (Eds. N. Ginsburg & R. Ginsburg). Yale University.

40 Concluding Remarks on Ways to Identify Defenses in Athletes

There needs to be an alternative to the current cognitive behavioral paradigm in sport psychology. Depth sport psychology provides this alternative by providing the athlete and the practitioner a chance to explore the underlying dynamics in the athlete's unconscious. A psychoanalytic or psychodynamic approach contrasts sharply with the current approach in sport psychology. Rather than promising a facile, quick and simple fix to the athlete's performance enhancement, depth sport psychology takes a more sober and realistic stance in these matters. The future will undoubtedly provide a more fully integrated approach combining techniques to remove symptoms along with insight and psychological growth, but for now, it is necessary to emphasize and outline how the past influences the athlete.

This book has demonstrated that athletes use naturally developed defenses which lie within their unconscious and these defenses enable them to cope with significant internal and external stress felt during competitive play. The athlete's use of their defenses is an uncharted territory of study, and for any ambitious graduate student, the area is wide open and in need of research.

I have tried to show how the more primitive defenses are a sign of early childhood losses and are often problematic. The chapters on denial with the aging athlete, drug use as acting out, grandiosity, depersonalization in a golfer and autistic fantasies in a long-distance swimmer are good examples of the use of the primitive defenses. Other primitive and maladaptive defenses commonly seen in athletes include somatization, superstitious behavior, regression on teams and scapegoating on teams.

The neurotic defenses I outlined in the book include the displacement of the athlete's anger into spouses, reaction formation seen in Asian athletes and the undoing defenses of choking. Other neurotic or mid-level defenses include overcompensation, dissociation and the repression of aggression, all of which serve a purpose, but if overused, lead to problems.

The mature defenses athletes use are usually helpful and a sign of mental health. These would include self-observation to gain perspective

Concluding Remarks on Ways to Identify Defenses in Athletes 189

and self-control, affiliation and anticipation or the ability to plan for all contingencies. The use of humor, asceticism, suppression and the ability to sublimate instincts into sports are all forms of mature defenses and ought to be encouraged and reinforced when seen. Some mature defenses are more problematic such as counterphobia and altruistic surrender and are examples of a good defense that is at times taken too far.

In the following sections, I will outline how to identify the presence of a defense and what to do about it when you see it.

The primitive defenses are as follows:

1 Denial: This is evidenced when an injured player wants to return to play too soon, an older player refuses to retire or when an athlete fails to see they are overworking to the point of injury. This suggests that they may be using the defense of denial. It is recommended that the therapist gently confront the player with your impression of their denial and support them over time to help them to get beyond the use of this primitive defense.
2 Acting out: When an athlete is using drugs to cope with stress, this is a sign of impulsive acting out and shows an inability to master emotions. When seen, the therapist needs to help the athlete to explore the causes underlying the drug use, and it will often show that the athlete is thus far ill-equipped to tolerate prolonged feelings of anxiety, anger or pain. An exploration of the causes of this deficiency will prove to be helpful and reparative.
3 Self-idealization: This common defense in star athletes is displayed in a number of ways, including a cavalier attitude toward keeping appointments and superficial conversations that fail to go beyond surface topics. Milman called this trait "acquired situational narcissism." The request for strict adherence to the framework of the sessions (i.e., once or twice weekly sessions at a certain hour) will be appreciated by the athlete and will elicit in them more respect for the therapy process and more trust that the therapist knows what he or she is doing.
4 Depersonalization: This defense is often difficult to spot immediately, but if the therapist feels that the athlete is guarded or appears awkward, this may show depersonalization. Also, at intake, if a coach or parent suggests that the athlete is odd or standoffish, this may also be a sign of a depersonalized athlete. The process that seems useful is to provide a relaxed, nonjudgmental and lighthearted approach so that the athlete can relax and have the courage to discuss his feeling strange or odd. This defense is not unusual to see but often goes undiagnosed.
5 Autistic fantasy: Autistic fantasy, depersonalization and dissociation are similar and displayed by the shy, quiet, introspective athlete who chooses sports like marathon running, long-distance biking, swimming,

hiking or golf, sports that provide a sense of isolation and where you are not a part of a team. It may not be necessary to intervene other than to make sure you do not pathologize the athlete. It is wise to emphasize the way introspective people are often creative and kind.

The neurotic defenses are as follows:

1 Displacement: When a frustrated athlete takes out his anger at home, this is displacement, and when used, the spouse suffers greatly and the marriage is put in jeopardy. When the sport psychologist sees this happening, you need to inform them that it puts the marriage in danger. You also must help them to deal with the reasons for their sport-related frustrations and why they hesitate to express things directly.
2 Repression: If an athlete seems unaware of normally felt emotional states such as anger or anxiety, it is possible that they are repressing them. This can be a valuable defense and may be one reason that South Korean women remain so poised as they compete on the LPGA. The only time one would want to change this ability is if the athlete is habitually repressing fatigue and pain and this is pushing them toward burnout or injury. If this is the case, begin to talk to them about the feeling they seem to be repressing and how valuable rest and recovery is.
3 Undoing defense: If an athlete has a pattern of choking, this may be due to the defense of undoing whereby they undo their success. The therapist needs to engage the athlete in a discussion of what conflicts, guilt and distortions they might have about success. The undoing defense is described as canceling out or making amends for some behavior they perceive to be wrong or guilt inducing. A good example of undoing seen in golf is the way Greg Norman became known for giving up leads, the most dramatic was when he gave up a six-shot lead to Nick Faldo in the Masters. When an athlete has this problem, it is best to help them to discuss reasons of guilt about winning. They will initially deny this, but over time, if one persists, the truth will often be revealed and be related to fears of separating from others or feeling undeserving.
4 Overcompensation: When you observe any successful highly driven athlete who perseveres and tolerates pain and repeated failure, chances are you are observing the defense of overcompensation or an effort to overcome feelings of inferiority by becoming highly skilled in one area. This is a valuable source of motivation, but without an awareness of the underlying dynamic, the athlete will be unable to feel any pride or peace and will remain overly driven until they get sick or injured. The way to help them to achieve pride is to explore with them their underlying feelings of inferiority. Many athletes fear that if they gain pride, they will lose their drive to win but this is never the case.

5 Intellectualization: Many educated and bright athletes use intellectualization as a defense. They will often complain that they "overthink" while playing. The therapist needs to ask them to discuss the feelings that underly the competitive moment and one often observes conflicts about aggression or winning.
6 Isolation: When an athlete is able to remain eerily calm when under great pressure, they may be employing the defense of isolation. This defense is defined as the ability to detach emotion from an idea or an event rendering the affect unconscious. This allows them to play in an unemotional state and is of enormous benefit in some sports like golf, diving or rifle shooting. One does not want to intervene with these athletes, but with other sports like boxing, tennis, football or basketball, the athlete needs to enlist emotions. In these cases, one ought to discuss the reason for flat affect in these settings and give permission to the athlete to be expressive.
7 Dissociation: If one observes the athlete behaving in an uncharacteristic way or if they admit to changing personality in certain settings, this may be evidence of the use of dissociation. This defense is defined as the temporary but drastic modification of identity used to avoid pain, anxiety or distress. This is a powerful and very effective defense used by long-distance runners or other endurance athletes. In the film "The Bourne Identity," the backstory involves the manner in which a special branch of the military produces dissociation in its applicants in order to turn them into fearless, ruthless killing machines. Needless to say, one is not able to train athletes in this way, but if you encounter an endurance athlete who employs this defense, one ought not try to change it because it is doubtful you will be able to replace it with something that works as well.
8 Reaction formation: When you encounter an athlete who is consistently friendly, smiling and sweet, you may be seeing someone using reaction formation. This defense is defined as the unconscious tendency to deal with an unacceptable impulse such as aggression by only permitting the expression of its opposite. This is not a helpful playing defense for athletes who need to be in touch with their aggression. One needs to teach them how to replace this defense with one which permits aggression to be felt. I will often promote the defense called identification with the aggressor. See Chapter 15 for a detailed description of how this is done.
9 Repression: When you see an athlete being self-defeating, this could be a sign they are using repression. This defense is the withholding from conscious awareness a feeling or desire that the athlete is conflicted about. Aggression is often repressed by athletes. This is also an unproductive defense for athletes, and it will be necessary to carefully explore with them their unconscious conflicts. As with all of these defenses, it takes time and effort to uncover the inner conflicts which are repressed, but this may be the only way to help them overcome self-defeat.

192 Odds and Ends

The mature adaptive defenses are as follows:

1 The counterphobic defense: Athletes such as NASCAR drivers, gamblers and mountaineers, those who face death every day, probably employ a counterphobic motive. Counterphobia is based upon fear but rather than avoiding the frightening situation, the person seeks out the setting that is most frightening. It is similar to the repetition compulsions talked about previously. Athletes who are compelled to compete without rest as I described in Chapter 24 need help in gaining insight into this extreme motivation. Counterphobia is often considered an adaptive defense since it displays courage, but when taken to extreme, it can be dangerous. Usually, one has a chance to delve into this defense after injury or illness where it is relatively easy to demonstrate the recklessness shown, and at this point, the athlete is more motivated to change.
2 Self-observation: The defense is defined as the ability to see oneself realistically and without distortion or devaluation. I have never encountered an athlete who came in with this high-level defense. All athletes will be saddled with some kind of distorted thinking about themselves which produces performance issues and why the sport psychologist is called upon. Self-observation is the goal one works toward. It is done with the therapist's instinctive feedback as the athlete presents distorted perceptions and the therapist responds with reality feedback.
3 Altruistic surrender: Charity, volunteerism and heroic sacrifice are all forms of altruism and usually considered to be prosocial and the central tenet to many world religions. However, when taken to extremes, it becomes a problem. This defense is marked with psychoanalytic controversy (see Chapter 26 for details). Giving is good but giving too much results in fatigue and resentment, even if the resentment is repressed. Anna Freud defined altruistic surrender as a devotional giving to another and considered the defense to be maladaptive. The object relations therapists align altruism with the presence of a false self. An athlete who is a team player displays altruism, but there must be a balance between self-sacrifice and taking your own shot at glory. When a player seems to be willing to admit to giving balls away and passing too much, they may be stuck with altruistic surrender. The treatment involves discussing this pattern of self-sacrifice and exploring the underlying fears of taking shots and perhaps failing.
4 Anticipation defense. When an athlete discusses a pre-game strategy to help themselves cope with game time emotions, this shows that they have acquired the defense of anticipation. This defense is defined as the realistic planning for a future event which may cause discomfort. A good example of anticipation was when Djokovic realized the crowd would be pulling for Roger Federer in the Wimbledon finals and so he rehearsed a strategy which prompted him to hear the crowd silence as

Concluding Remarks on Ways to Identify Defenses in Athletes 193

cheers. To develop the anticipation defense in an athlete, one needs to discuss with them in detail all things that could create emotional distress before and during a game (i.e., getting behind early, playing with the lead, bad calls, rain delays). These strategies then need to be written out and memorized by the player.

5 Asceticism: The defense of asceticism refers to the elimination of pleasurable pursuits in order to achieve pride through renunciation. To get to the top, athletes need to renounce many pleasures, be they social, dietary, or physical. The ability to renounce these activities is especially problematic for teenage athletes who feel the pull to hang out with their friends rather than get to bed early in order to work out the next morning. One way to encourage the development of this defense is to cite examples. Athletes like Tiger Woods, Michael Jordan or Pistol Pete Maravich are all exemplars of some who sacrificed pleasures in order to grow and gain fame and fortune.

6 Humor: This defense is defined as the ability to express taboo feelings without bringing undo discomfort to the self or to others. The value of this skill to society is demonstrated by the salaries received by comedians like Jerry Seinfeld, Jim Carrey or Adam Sandler. It is easy to observe when an athlete has this skill by the easy way they joke around in the session. This is a skill to be reinforced and enjoyed by the therapist, but if joking is constantly used by the athlete to avoid deeper more meaningful topics, then it ought to be confronted.

7 Suppression: Suppression is defined as the ability to temporarily avoid thinking about disturbing problems, ideas or feelings. This defense is subtle in appearance but an extremely valuable defense for athletes since it enables them to avoid getting ahead of themselves by fantasizing victory. To observe suppression, it is often necessary to watch the athlete perform while under pressure. If they seem unflappable, calm and poised, no matter what the pressure faced, it is likely they are using suppression. As I indicated in Chapter 30, many Asian athletes seem to possess this defense. To train the athlete in the ability to suppress and "stay in the moment," there are drills I have developed that are explained in detail in Chapter 30.

8 Sublimation: This defense involves the channeling of either aggressive or sexual instinct into a socially sanctioned activity. Sublimation, along with self-observation, is a hallmark of mental health. Sports is a setting which allows for and encourages the sublimation of aggression, but many athletes do not use this defense due to conflicts about aggression. As one works to resolve self-defeating conflicts in the athlete, it is also then necessary to encourage the free expression of aggression. This will enhance the athlete's ability to enjoy their sport and also improve their performance. One can use expressive language and animated body language with them and encourage them to do the same in session.

In this book, I have explained why an awareness of the athlete's use of their defense mechanisms will help their performance by developing an understanding of how their mind works. I have also tried to show why their defenses sometimes breakdown. Historically, defense mechanisms have been categorized into immature, neurotic and mature defenses and I have followed that rubric. You will also have noticed that surprisingly, some primitive defenses like self-idealization, autistic fantasy and dissociation can actually be quite helpful to the competitive athlete, especially endurance athletes. Conversely, some of the more mature defenses like intellectualization, reaction formation and altruistic surrender are clearly damaging to the athlete's performance. In this concluding chapter, I detailed a methodology to help both the athlete and the sport psychologist to observe the presence of defenses and how to improve on them.

> For the field of sport psychology to remain relevant, a paradigm shift is needed which allows the sport psychologist and the athlete to explore the inner recesses of the mind, the place Freud called the unconscious.
>
> There are underlying reasons that psychoanalysis is usually resisted. The cognitive behavioral therapist will resist this paradigm shift because to become a psychoanalyst one needs an additional four years of training, part of which involves class work and part involves undergoing a personal analysis of 3–4 times per week on the analytic couch for those four years. This is the only way to develop an understanding of how the mind actually works. Sport psychology training needs to include classwork on psychoanalytic theory as well as a requirement to engage is some form of psychodynamic therapy. The reason that psychoanalysis is resisted by athletes is that many abhor dependency and see the therapeutic bond as a trap and an insult. In addition, the awareness that our life is dictated by forces within our unconscious and not in our control is a great narcissistic blow. Athletes and people in general resist feelings of dependency, insight, and change. That is the reason our defenses have been established and why they are so strong. They are built to protect us from any anxiety we may feel. Furthermore, no one wants to enter the dark, scarey murky swamp of the unconscious but the truth is that for athletes to improve, resolve symptoms, fulfill potential and experience their fair measure of joy, the childhood demons within the unconscious must be faced. And if not, it is the demons of the past that will dictate the outcome of games and of careers.

Index

acceptance therapy 14
The Achievement Zone (Murphy) 158
Aching for Beauty: Footbinding in China (Ping) 82
acting, defined 29
acting out 6, 12, 189; in athletes 29–33; primitive defenses 189
Adaptation to Life (Vaillant) 80
Adler, Alfred 8, 86–87
affect defense: in athletes 99–102; isolation of 99–102
age: and denial 24–27; weakening of defense mechanisms with 154–156
aggression: direct expression of 81; passive 7; and sublimation 144–146; and winning 144–146
aggressor: identification with 7–8; as a tool to suppress anxiety 73–76
aging athlete: and anxiety during competition 154–155; denial mechanisms in 24–27
Agronin, M. 155
alexithymia 62, 65
Allen, Woody 122
altruism 10; defined 125, 181; European athletes' use of 181; mature defenses 10
altruistic surrender: defense 4, 10, 125–128, 192; mature defenses 10; in sports 125–128
anchoring techniques 40
anger 1, 3, 157, 173, 182, 184, 188–190; and denial 26; direct expression of 81; displacement of 78–80; as part of competitive sports 140; and passive aggression 7; and somatization 65; and sublimation 11; suppressing 63, 107, 111

Annie Hall (film) 122
anticipation: defined 10, 129; in golf 10; as mature defense 10
anticipation defense 10, 13, 15, 39, 192–193; defined 129; as definitive pregame routine 129–131; effectiveness of 129–130; and "Murphy's Law" 129
anxiety 2, 4, 14, 19, 21, 29, 30, 32, 39, 51, 140; competitive 141–143; identification with aggressor as tool to suppress 73–76; management 12; as part of competitive sports 140
Any Given Sunday (film) 111
apathetic depression 176
The Art of War (Sun Tzu) 129
asceticism 10, 12, 13, 193; defined 133; in longdistance cyclist 133–136; mature defenses 10
Asian athletes: and philosophy of Confucius 81; repression and reaction formation in 81–84
athletes: acting out/impulsivity/drug use in 29–33; aging 24–27; Asian 81–84; choking 94–98; competing, reasons for 118–121; defense mechanisms used by 6–11; doubting in 90–93; emotional breakdowns in 17–22; giving away leads 125–128; grandiosity in 34–37; identifying defenses in 188–194; and intellectualization defense 90–93; isolation of affect defense in 99–102; mental health *vs.* mental illness in 166–170; narcissism in 34–37; perfectionism/splitting defense in 46–49; problem of prescription drug use in 172–174; regressed

196 *Index*

51–54; self-idealization in 34–37; somatization in 60–66; superstitious behavior used by regressed 51–54; using humor to cope with stress 138–140; value of selfobservation for 122–124
autistic fantasy 7, 23, 44, 189–190; defined 42; in a long-distance swimmer 42–45; primitive defenses 189–190
autogenics 14, 112
Aykroyd, Dan 139

Barkley, Charles 109
Becker, Ernest 24
Bernays, Edward 47
Biles, Simone 17, 18, 166, 167
Bion, Wilfred 7, 55, 56, 57
The Bourne Identity (film) 191
Boyle, Danny 96
Bryant, Kobe 166
Buddhism 100, 133, 135, 157, 159, 164

Carrey, Jim 11, 139, 193
Catlett, J. 46
Challengers (film) 151
Chariots of Fire (film) 165
"The Childhood of the Artist" (Greenacre) 61
choking 8, 95–96, 107, 113, 146
Clemens, Roger 74
cognitive developmental theory 12
compartmentalization 99, 142
competitive anxiety 31; ability to handle 124; coping with 157; managing 177; suppression used to manage 141–143
Confucianism 81
Confucius 81
Coping and Defending (Haan) 12
coping mechanism: "higher power" as 162–165; in sports 162–165
coping skills 13, 33; defense mechanisms 12–16; teaching 12–16
coping with stress 138–140
counterphobia 118–121; mature defenses 9–10
counterphobic defense 9–10, 192; defined 118; unconscious 119
countertransference 34
Covid pandemic 135
Cradles of Eminence (Goertzel and Goertzel) 9, 86

Cramer, Phebe 13
Csikszentmihalyi, Mihaly 144, 157
cultural differences in use of defenses 180–186
Cultural Revolution 100

defense mechanisms 12, 13, 14; acting out 6; addressed prior to teaching coping skills 12–16; autistic fantasy 7; denial 6; dissociation 7; idealization of the self 6–7; identification with the aggressor 7–8; identification with the victim 8; passive aggression 7; regression 7; somatization 8; thought blocking 7; used by athletes 6–11; weakening with age 154–156
defenses: cultural differences in use of 180–186; identifying, in athletes 188–194; *see also specific types*
definitive pregame routine: anticipation defense as 129–131
denial 6, 12, 13, 23, 24, 26, 189; and age 24–27; and anger 26; defined 24; mechanisms in aging athlete 24–27; primitive defenses 189
depersonalization 23, 39–40, 41, 139, 189; defined 38; in a golfer 38–41; primitive defenses 189
depression 17–19, 35, 123, 166, 183–184; apathetic 176; masked/endogenous 60, 65; and pharmacology 167; psychotic 172; used as a defense by athletes fearing failure 176–179
Deutsch, Felix 60, 94
Deutsch, Helene 118, 184
displacement 8, 190; of anger into a spouse 78–80; defined 78; neurotic defenses 8, 190
dissociation 2, 4, 7, 172, 188–189; defined 7; as neurotic defense 191; in sports 103–106
dissociation defense 7, 12, 38, 103, 189–190, 191
doubting: in athletes 90–93; and intellectualization defense 90–93
Drugs and the Athlete (Wadler) 173
drug use, in athletes 29–33

Ehlers-Danlos syndrome (EDS) 109–110
Eisold, Kenneth 57

Ellis, A. 1, 13
emotional breakdowns, in athletes 17–22
English Premier League 11, 138
European athletes, and altruism 181

Fairbairn, Ronald 105, 154
Faist, Mike 151
"Family Matters" show 44
fatigue 21, 29, 30
Fearless (film) 121
Ferrari (film) 121
Festinger, Leon 95
Firestone, R. 46
For Love of the Game (film) 124
Forrest Gump (film) 111
Frankl, Victor 154; *Man's Search for Meaning* 25–26
Franklin, Benjamin 184
Freud, Anna 2, 10, 13, 29, 162
Freud, Sigmund 2, 42, 47–48, 89, 94, 114, 154, 162, 168; *Repeating, Remembering and Working Through* 30
Fukada, Kaori 184

Gabbard, G. 150
Gilligan, Carol 185; *In a Different Voice: Psychological Theory and Women's Development* 185
Goertzel, M.: *Cradles of Eminence* 9, 86
Goertzel, V.: *Cradles of Eminence* 9, 86
golf: as an example of repression 112–115; yips in 112–115
golfer: amateur 91, 95, 150; Asian wave of 83; depersonalization in 38–41; Korean 100; LPGA 86–89; professional 46–47, 95–96, 126, 134–135; reaction formation in 107–108; and yips 104
grandiosity 10, 23, 34–37; in the athlete 34–37
Greenacre, Phyllis 61; *"The Childhood of the Artist"* 61
Green Book (film) 126
Grotstein, James 46, 67

Haan, Norma 12; *Coping and Defending* 12
higher power as coping mechanism in sports 162–165
Hogan, Ben 7

Huizinga, Johan 144
humor 11, 12, 13, 15, 39; athletes using to cope with stress 138–140; defined 138; mature defenses 11
humor defense 193

idealization of self 6–7
identification: with the aggressor 7–8; with aggressor as tool to suppress anxiety 73–76; with the victim 8
immature defenses 4, 6, 19, 23
impulsivity, in athletes 29–33
In a Different Voice: Psychological Theory and Women's Development (Gilligan) 185
inferiority: organ 86; turning into superiority in LPGA Golfer 86–89
intellectualization 9, 12, 191; defined 90; neurotic defenses 9, 191
intellectualization defense: doubting in athletes and 90–93
isolation 9, 99, 191; of affect defense in athletes 99–102; neurotic defenses 9, 191

Jackson, Reggie 74
Jordan, Michael 193
Joslin, Roger 159, 164; *Running the Spiritual Path* 159

Kelly, George 31
Kennedy, John 138
King Richard (film) 89
Kirschner, Gordon 176
Klein, Melanie 46, 154
Koepka, Brooks 74
Krasner, Leonard 13
Kubler-Ross, Elizabeth 24
Kuhn, Thomas 1

Ladies Professional Golf Association 11, 86–89
LaMotta, Jake 10
logotherapy 25, 154
longdistance cyclist: asceticism in 133–136; renunciation of pleasure in 133–136
long-distance swimmer, autistic fantasies in 42–45
LPGA golfer: turning inferiority into superiority in 86–89

198 Index

Magnetic Resonance Imaging (MRIs) 61
Mahler, Margaret 51, 158
Man's Search for Meaning (Frankl) 25–26
Maravich, Pistol Pete 193
masked/endogenous depression 60, 65
masochism 10, 125, 126
Mastroianni, Marcello 26
mature adaptive defenses 192–193; altruistic surrender 192; anticipation defense 192–193; asceticism 193; counterphobic defense 192; humor 193; selfobservation 192; sublimation 193; suppression 193
mature defenses 4, 6, 15, 20; altruism and altruistic surrender 10; anticipation 10; asceticism 10; counterphobia 9–10; humor 11; self-observation 10; sublimation 11; suppression 11
McDougall, Joyce 61, 62
McIlroy, Rory 96
meditation/prayer as way to find zone 157–160
Mental Health in Elite Sport: Applied Perspectives from Across the Globe 180
mental health *vs.* mental illness in athletes 166–170
multiple personality disorder 39
Murakami, Haruki 43; *What I Talk About When I Talk About Running: A Memoir* 43; *The Wind-Up Bird Chronicle* 43
Murphy, Shane 158; *The Achievement Zone* 158
Murphy's Law 10
Myers, J. 30
Myers, Mike 139

narcissism, in athlete 34–37
National Basketball Association 57
Netflix 22
neurotic defenses 4, 8–9, 190–191; displacement 8, 190; dissociation 191; intellectualization 9, 191; isolation 9, 191; overcompensation 8–9, 190; rationalization 9; reaction formation 9, 191; repression 8, 190, 191; undoing 8; undoing defense 190

New York Post 94
Nixdorf, I. 181
Norman, Greg 190

O'Connor, Josh 151
Osaka, Naomi 17, 18, 166, 167
overcompensation 8–9, 86–89, 190; defined 86; neurotic defenses 8–9, 190

passive aggression 7; and anger 7
perfectionism defense 23, 46; in athletes 46–49
Personal Construct Theory 31
Ping, Wang 82; *Aching for Beauty: Footbinding in China* 82
positive self-talk 12, 14, 25, 52, 54, 63, 107, 130, 157
prescription drug use, problem in athletes 172–174
primitive defense 6–8, 26, 189–190; acting out 189; autistic fantasy 189–190; denial 189; depersonalization 189; selfidealization 189
professional soccer team, regression in 55–59
professional teams: and psychoanalysis 57; scapegoating and splitting in 67–71; sport psychologists 56–57
psychoanalysis 3, 26, 122, 125, 133, 157, 158, 166
psychotic depression 172

rational emotive therapy (RET) 12, 14, 112
rationalization 9, 12, 91, 92; neurotic defenses 9
reaction formation 9, 107–111, 191; in Asian athletes 81–84; neurotic defenses 9, 191
Reagan, Ronald 138
regressed athlete, and superstitious behavior 51–54
regression 7, 23, 51, 53; defined 55; in professional soccer team 55–59
Reich, Wilhem 108
relaxation therapy 14, 19, 107
renunciation of pleasure in longdistance cyclist 133–136
Repeating, Remembering and Working Through (Freud) 30

repression 8, 12, 13, 39, 190, 191; in Asian athletes 81–84; defined 81, 82, 112; neurotic defenses 8, 190, 191; yips in golf as an example of 112–115
Roberts, B. 30
Roosevelt, Teddy 86
Rotella, B. 13
Routledge Handbook of Mental Health in Elite Sport 166
Rudolph, Wilma 86
Running the Spiritual Path (Joslin) 159

Salzman, L. 172
Sandler, Adam 11, 193
Santos, Jose 134
scapegoating 67–68, 70; in professional teams 67–71
Seinfeld, Jerry 193
self-acceptance 27
self-idealization 6–7, 189; in the athlete 34–37; defined 34; primitive defenses 189
self-observation 10, 15; defined 122; mature defenses 10; value for athletes 122–124
self-observation defense 192
Seligman, Martin 167
sexual impulse in sports 148–151
sexuality 2, 11, 148, 149
sexual sublimation 148, 150
Shafer, R. 48
Short, Martin 139
short-term interventions 13
Skinner, B.F. 2, 167
Skype 44
somatization 8, 23, 64–65, 82; and anger 65; in athletes 60–66; defined 60
Sorenstam, Anika 41
splitting defense, in athletes 46–49
splitting, in professional teams 67–71
sport psychology 1–2, 12, 14, 194
sports: altruistic surrender in 125–128; dissociation in 103–106; higher power as coping mechanism in 162–165; sublimation of sexual impulse in 148–151
spouse: displacement of anger into 78–80
The Strange Case of Dr. Jekyll and Mr. Hyde (Stevenson) 39
Steinbrenner, George 57

Stevenson, Robert Louis: *The Strange Case of Dr. Jekyll and Mr. Hyde* 39
stress: athletes using humor to cope with 138–140; competitive 2, 12, 18, 52; emotional 61, 103; extreme 7, 60; posttraumatic 103
Suarez-Orozco, Marcelo 184–185
sublimation 11, 12, 27; and aggression 144–146; and anger 11; defined 144; mature defenses 11; sexual 148, 150; of sexual impulse in sports 148–151; and winning 144–146
sublimation defense 11, 193
Sullivan, Harry Stack 113
Sun Tzu 129; *The Art of War* 129
superiority: turning inferiority in LPGA Golfer 86–89
superstitions 23
superstitious behavior, used by regressed athlete 51–54
suppression defense 11, 12, 15, 39, 182, 193; defined 141; mature defenses 11; used to manage competitive anxiety 141–143

tension, as part of competitive sports 140
Terr, Lenore 17, 104, 144
Thoreau, Henry David 133; *Walden; Life in the Woods* 133
Those Wrecked by Success (Freud) 94, 96–97, 176
thought blocking 7
Tornatore, Giuseppe 26
Tyson, Mike 166

undoing defense 8, 94–98, 190; neurotic defenses 190

Valliant, George 13, 42, 125–126, 144, 154; *Adaptation to Life* 80
value of selfobservation, for athletes 122–124
visualization 12, 14, 19

Wadler, Gary 173; *Drugs and the Athlete* 173
Walden; Life in the Woods (Thoreau) 133
weakening of defense mechanisms with age 154–156

What I Talk About When I Talk About Running: A Memoir (Murakami) 43
Why Has Bodhi Dharma Left for the East (film) 160
Williams, Nancy Mc 118, 142
Williams, Richard 22
Williams, Steve 129
The Wind-Up Bird Chronicle (Murakami) 43

Winnicott, Donald 10
winning: and aggression 144–146; and sublimation 144–146
Woods, Tiger 7, 44, 56, 193
World War II 183
Wurmser, Leon 172

yawning 34–35
yips: in golf as example of repression 112–115; and golfer 104

For Product Safety Concerns and Information please contact our EU representative GPSR@taylorandfrancis.com
Taylor & Francis Verlag GmbH, Kaufingerstraße 24, 80331 München, Germany